TRACING YOUR YORKSHIRE ANCESTORS ON THE INTERNET

FAMILY HISTORY FROM PEN & SWORD BOOKS

Birth, Marriage & Death Records
The Family History Web Directory
Tracing British Battalions on the Somme
Tracing Great War Ancestors
Tracing History Through Title Deeds
Tracing Secret Service Ancestors
Tracing the Rifle Volunteers
Tracing Your Air Force Ancestors
Tracing Your Ancestors
Tracing Your Ancestors from 1066 to 1837
Tracing Your Ancestors Through Death Records – Second Edition
Tracing Your Ancestors Through Family Photographs
Tracing Your Ancestors Through Letters and Personal Writings
Tracing Your Ancestors Using DNA
Tracing Your Ancestors Using the Census
Tracing your Ancestors Using the UK Timeline
Tracing Your Ancestors: Cambridgeshire, Essex, Norfolk and Suffolk
Tracing Your Aristocratic Ancestors
Tracing Your Army Ancestors
Tracing Your Army Ancestors – Third Edition
Tracing Your Birmingham Ancestors
Tracing Your Black Country Ancestors
Tracing Your Boer War Ancestors
Tracing Your British Indian Ancestors
Tracing Your Canal Ancestors
Tracing Your Channel Islands Ancestors
Tracing Your Church of England Ancestors
Tracing Your Criminal Ancestors
Tracing Your Docker Ancestors
Tracing Your East Anglian Ancestors
Tracing Your East End Ancestors
Tracing Your Family History on the Internet
Tracing Your Female Ancestors
Tracing Your First World War Ancestors
Tracing Your Freemason, Friendly Society and Trade Union Ancestors
Tracing Your Georgian Ancestors, 1714–1837
Tracing Your Glasgow Ancestors
Tracing Your Great War Ancestors: The Gallipoli Campaign
Tracing Your Great War Ancestors: The Somme
Tracing Your Great War Ancestors: Ypres
Tracing Your Huguenot Ancestors
Tracing Your Insolvent Ancestors
Tracing Your Irish Family History on the Internet
Tracing Your Jewish Ancestors
Tracing Your Jewish Ancestors – Second Edition
Tracing Your Labour Movement Ancestors
Tracing Your Legal Ancestors
Tracing Your Liverpool Ancestors
Tracing Your Liverpool Ancestors – Second Edition
Tracing Your London Ancestors
Tracing Your Medical Ancestors
Tracing Your Merchant Navy Ancestors
Tracing Your Northern Ancestors
Tracing Your Northern Irish Ancestors
Tracing Your Northern Irish Ancestors – Second Edition
Tracing Your Oxfordshire Ancestors
Tracing Your Pauper Ancestors
Tracing Your Police Ancestors
Tracing Your Potteries Ancestors
Tracing Your Pre-Victorian Ancestors
Tracing Your Prisoner of War Ancestors: The First World War
Tracing Your Railway Ancestors
Tracing Your Roman Catholic Ancestors
Tracing Your Royal Marine Ancestors
Tracing Your Rural Ancestors
Tracing Your Scottish Ancestors
Tracing Your Second World War Ancestors
Tracing Your Servant Ancestors
Tracing Your Service Women Ancestors
Tracing Your Shipbuilding Ancestors
Tracing Your Tank Ancestors
Tracing Your Textile Ancestors
Tracing Your Twentieth-Century Ancestors
Tracing Your Welsh Ancestors
Tracing Your West Country Ancestors
Tracing Your Yorkshire Ancestors
Writing Your Family History
Your Irish Ancestors

Tracing Your Yorkshire Ancestors on the Internet

A Guide for Family Historians

RACHEL BELLERBY

Pen & Sword
FAMILY HISTORY

First published in Great Britain in 2024 by
PEN AND SWORD FAMILY HISTORY
An imprint of
Pen & Sword Books Ltd
Yorkshire – Philadelphia

Copyright © Rachel Bellerby, 2024

ISBN 978 1 39905 162 0

The right of Rachel Bellerby to be identified as Author of this work has been asserted by her in accordance with the Copyright, Designs and Patents Act 1988.

A CIP catalogue record for this book is available from the British Library. All rights reserved. No part of this book may be reproduced or transmitted in any form or by any means, electronic or mechanical including photocopying, recording or by any information storage and retrieval system, without permission from the Publisher in writing.

The publisher has no responsibility for the persistence or accuracy of URLs for any external or third-party internet websites referred to in this book, and does not guarantee that any content on such websites is, or will remain, accurate or appropriate.

Typeset by Mac Style
Printed and bound in the UK by CPI Group (UK) Ltd,
Croydon, CR0 4YY.

Pen & Sword Books Limited incorporates the imprints of After the Battle, Atlas, Archaeology, Aviation, Discovery, Family History, Fiction, History, Maritime, Military, Military Classics, Politics, Select, Transport, True Crime, Air World, Frontline Publishing, Leo Cooper, Remember When, Seaforth Publishing, The Praetorian Press, Wharncliffe Local History, Wharncliffe Transport, Wharncliffe True Crime and White Owl.

For a complete list of Pen & Sword titles please contact:
PEN & SWORD BOOKS LIMITED
47 Church Street, Barnsley, South Yorkshire, S70 2AS, England
E-mail: enquiries@pen-and-sword.co.uk
Website: www.pen-and-sword.co.uk
or
PEN AND SWORD BOOKS
1950 Lawrence Road, Havertown, PA 19083, USA
E-mail: uspen-and-sword@casematepublishers.com
Website: www.penandswordbooks.com

CONTENTS

Glossary		vi
Introduction		vii
Chapter 1	What's Held Where?	1
Chapter 2	Vital Records for Birth, Marriage and Death	18
Chapter 3	Home Life: The Census and House History	34
Chapter 4	Education and Occupations	45
Chapter 5	Tough Times: Ill Health, Poverty and Crime	62
Chapter 6	Leisure and Religion	71
Chapter 7	Tracing Your Female Ancestors	84
Chapter 8	Emigration, Immigration and 'Strays'	94
Chapter 9	Working with Others: Societies, Social Networking and Volunteering	107
Chapter 10	Adding Colour to Your Research	122
Acknowledgements		136
Index		137

GLOSSARY

Blog	Short For 'Web Log' – An Online Diary
BMD	Births, Marriages and Deaths
Cloud	An Online Data Storage Area
FHS	Family History Society
GEDCOM	A File Format (Short for Genealogical Data Communication)
GRO	General Register Office
IGI	International Genealogical Index
MI	Monumental Inscription
PDF	Portable Document Format
TNA	The National Archives (UK)
URL	Website Address
WYAS	West Yorkshire Archive Service

INTRODUCTION

When the first of these Pen & Sword *Tracing Ancestors on The Internet* guides were published, online research was still seen as something that required at least some specialist skills and equipment – and the comparatively few resources available online at the time reflected that.

Two decades on, family historians – along with the rest of the population – have become much more computer literate; now, being able to access large portions of family history research material online has become something of the 'norm'. That said, such resources are only accessible at the click of a mouse and keyboard thanks to the determined efforts of volunteers and employees across the UK and further afield who have transcribed, scanned and digitised these treasures.

This book explores and celebrates the rich variety of online material available to anyone researching their Yorkshire ancestors from anywhere around the world. I do mention at several points during the coming chapters that not everything is available online – and it probably never will be. There are millions of records to explore and enjoy via your computer or phone, but as things stand in the third decade of the twenty-first century, there are some resources we will never see online. But perhaps artificial intelligence will change that in years to come, who knows?

However you access your family history, please do support the archives, libraries, family and local history societies and museums across the county. The staff and volunteers at these organisations do a tremendous job, often working to tight budgets and time constraints, providing us eager researchers with information both online and on-site. Some of them have provided tips and wise words in the chapters that follow, generously sharing their expertise.

Some of the websites featured here have long URLs and so I have shortened these to Bitly links when it seemed that the long address would be very laborious to type into a search bar. The websites featured in the pages that follow were functional at the time of writing (July 2023). If they cease to function, look for the collection in question on a search engine such as Google, in case it has been moved to a new host platform, or try a site such as Wayback Machine, which may have cached an earlier version.

Enjoy your research and I hope you find many new and interesting Yorkshire ancestors.

Chapter 1

WHAT'S HELD WHERE?

In this chapter we'll take a look at Yorkshire's genealogical landscape, introducing the main record offices for each of the four areas of Yorkshire, before moving on to resources provided by the subscription-based giants of the family history world, the 'gateway sites' that can take you down many different research avenues, and finally, a selection of Yorkshire-wide sites that will be referred to many times throughout the book as we search out ancestors at home, work, in their leisure time and through the ups and downs of life.

How the County was Organised
Before being administratively reorganised in 1974, Yorkshire was the largest county in England. It was made up of three ridings: North, East and West, and divided into administrative units known as wapentakes. Two major places not included in the wapentake system were York and Kingston upon Hull.

After the 1974 reorganisation, many records were transferred to the new authorities, where they can still be found today. The main areas that hold information on both the modern county and the older Ridings are Cleveland, Humberside, North Yorkshire, South Yorkshire and West Yorkshire. We'll take a look at the online resources available for each of these areas below and for simplicity, unless otherwise specified, I'll be referring to the modern North, South, East and West Yorkshire when talking about places and place names.

Get Organised
Before you start or continue your online research, it's worth noting a few methods of good practice, if only because they can save hours of your time. When researching online it's all too easy to go 'down a rabbit hole'

and in your enthusiasm, forget not only how you got to a useful web page, but also how to find it again. As soon as you realise a website will be useful to you, either save it as a bookmark in your 'favourites' or keep a running document of useful sites.

Be aware also that no matter how popular or useful a particular page or website, the nature of online research means that not all information is available forever. It's all very well saving a weblink but this is no use should the site close down or move. Always screengrab information that you find very useful. If you do encounter a 'lost' site, try Wayback Machine (**http://archive.org**) or Web Archive (**www.webarchive.org.uk**), each of which regularly saves websites for posterity.

Even more than is the case with on-site research, care is needed when dealing with information that you find online. As with any historical investigation, weigh up how trustworthy your source is, corroborate or double-check the facts in more than one way, if possible, and use a primary source where available to corroborate. Remember, too, that despite the many records available to us, not all family history information is available online – in some cases you will have no choice but to carry out an on-site search, or to pay someone else to do so.

But most of all, enjoy your online genealogy adventure. We're so lucky that, thanks to the efforts of people all around over the world over the past few decades, we can access valuable information within just a few minutes that would at one time taken many hours and several on-site research trips to amass.

Although not everything can be found online, the hard work of volunteers over the decades has meant that previously difficult-to-access material can be easily accessed digitally. (© Arnaud Gangneux)

Key Record Offices

Before we move to the main record offices of North, South, East and West Yorkshire, the online gateway to the holdings of these, and thousands of other resources, is on the website of the UK National Archives, the official archive of the UK Government, and of England and Wales.

The key to the archive treasures of Yorkshire – and the rest of England – is the Discovery catalogue **https://discovery.nationalarchives.gov.uk** which lists 32 million descriptions of records held by the National Archives and more than 2,500 archives across the country. Happily, more than 9 million of these records can be explored online or downloaded. You can use this huge database right down to the level of entering an ancestor's name and a date range, then use the drop-down list to ask for 'all archives' rather than only the National Archives. The 'find an archive' allows you to enter 'Yorkshire' and get more than 180 repositories, including private collections with contact details to allow you to ask for permission to view.

> **Search tip**
> If you're searching with a phrase rather than a word, put the whole thing in quote marks when entering it into the search engine, e.g. 'Sowerby Bridge', to get results relating only to the exact phrase.

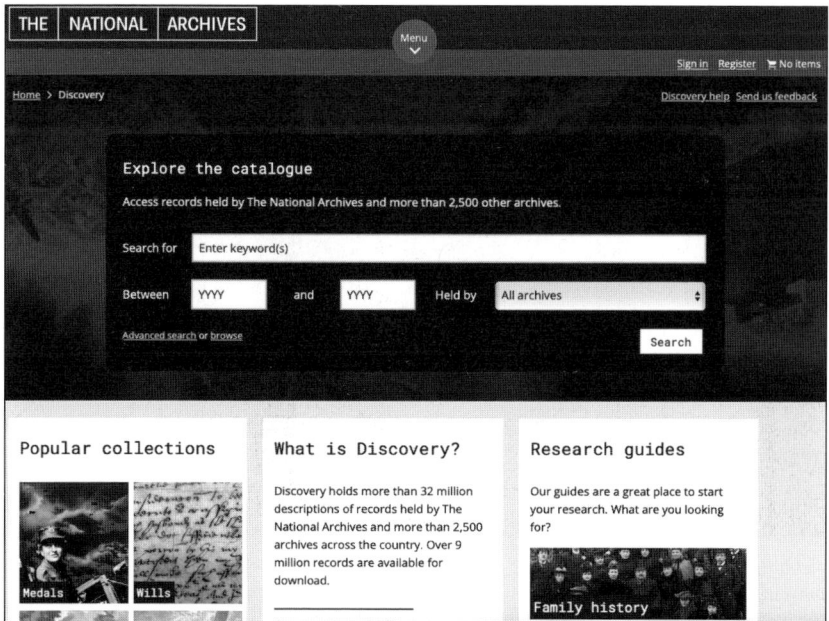

Exploring the Discovery catalogue.

The 'explore the catalogue' section on the home page is the main way to access the catalogues contained in the site. Search using keyword, archive repository or date, or alternatively use the advanced search to be more precise. If you're exploring a particular topic, the research guides are excellent and comprehensive, with information on where specific topics can be found. They make a great introduction to a subject if it's new to you, and at the time of writing, there are more than 350 guides available: **www.nationalarchives.gov.uk/help-with-your-research/research-guides/**. For online-only resources, simply tick the box at the top of the page.

In terms of county and city/town record offices, the East and North Yorkshire regions have county record offices at Beverley and Northallerton respectively, with the cities of Hull and York each having their own city archives. West Yorkshire is covered by the West Yorkshire Archive Service, which has branches in Bradford, Halifax, Huddersfield, Leeds and Wakefield. South Yorkshire has archives in Barnsley, Doncaster, Rotherham and Sheffield.

There are also two institutions that serve the whole county: the Borthwick Institute for Archives in York and the Yorkshire Archaeological Society in Leeds – see the following chapters for records on the various themes covered in different sections.

For all of the above, be sure to follow any that are relevant to your research on social media as particularly for online research, new accessions are often announced on Facebook and Twitter. Consider signing up to the organisation's blog and/or newsletter; with hundreds of new online collections available each year, these are a fun and easy way to keep abreast of developments in the field.

East Yorkshire
Records relating to East Yorkshire are cared for by East Riding Archives at the Treasure House in Beverley, and by Hull History Centre.

The main archive catalogue is at **www.eastriding.gov.uk/CalmView/** and this covers over 400,000 records that can be viewed at the Treasure House reading room, although you can make enquiries about having material copied and sent to you, depending upon the fragility of the document in question. The online catalogue has particularly detailed entries for some records such as Hull City Police, Broadgate Hospital and East Riding Quarter Sessions. At the time of writing, Treasure House was closed for building works, so check the website before travelling.

East Yorkshire Archives online can be accessed at **www.eastridingarchives.co.uk/archives-online/** including their What Was

Hull History Centre. (© C at TMM, CCASA 4.0)

Here app. The most recent additions include 'born digital' material such as Covid-19 recollections and local history club activities. These collections are the result of a wider goal to secure the permanent preservation of East Yorkshire digital archives through an automated digital repository, the Preservica system **https://eastriding.access.preservica.com**, which will help them remain accessible for generations to come. In keeping with the future generations theme, East Riding Blockdown is aimed at the 11–16 age group and is centred around a Minecraft world known as the 'Archiverse': **www.eastridingarchives.co.uk/archiverse**. Here, young people from the East Riding contributed their experiences from the Covid-19 pandemic to help future historians understand the world in the years around 2020.

Recently, it has become possible to go from a search result in the online catalogue to the relevant digital archive item in the Preservica universal access portal. Whilst the vast majority of the holdings are original hard copy archives, any available digital content will appear in catalogue search results with a clickable link through to the universal access portal. This means that if an archive video, oral history recording, or set of digital photographs exists, you can go straight to that item by clicking the 'Preservica Universal URL' link.

As the name suggests, Hull History Centre (**https://hullhistorycentre. org.uk/home.aspx**) is based in Hull, on Worship Street. The online catalogue **https://catalogue.hullhistorycentre.org.uk** has more than 300,000 items; the collections are particularly strong on Hull's maritime history, politics and campaigning, and key figures in the worlds of literature and drama. As well as exploring by keyword and advanced search, you can choose to incorporate or exclude any of the following repositories: Hull University Archives, Hull City Archives and Hull Local Studies Library.

Starting on the home page, the research guides are a good place to begin, with ideas for further study and links to various collections. You can also view 'stories from the strongroom' video talks by centre staff and follow @Hullhistorynews for new additions to the collections.

North Yorkshire

Based in Northallerton, North Yorkshire Archives collect, preserve and make available millions of historical records. The online catalogue **archivesunlocked.northyorks.gov.uk** contains descriptions of the records in their care and is regularly updated. This page is also home to ten guides to the collections, on topics including parish registers, architectural plans and enclosure awards. The house history guide includes a guide to using the North Riding Registry of Deeds, as well as overviews of a range of different record types for both buildings and owners/occupiers.

The shop page **http://archiveshop.northyorks.gov.uk** has details of the record office online research service, whereby staff can undertake research using their full range of records, including parish and Nonconformist registers of baptisms, marriages and burials, electoral registers, tithe maps and many other resources. You can pay per half-hour slot which, at the time of writing, is £19. As with all such services, the more initial information you can give (including details of unsuccessful searches), the more fruitful the outcome is likely to be.

South Yorkshire

As mentioned above, there are four gateways to the county archives of South Yorkshire: Barnsley, Doncaster, Rotherham and Sheffield. An excellent 130-page guide to the various materials available can be found at **https://bit.ly/491WT1y**. Do bear in mind that this was produced more than ten years ago, although it still gives a good overview of what's available where and mentions that for South Yorkshire ancestors, your search may also take you to Derbyshire, Lichfield and Nottinghamshire archives, because of changing boundaries over the centuries.

Barnsley

Barnsley Archives, whose records go back to the 1150s, is accessed via a hub page **www.experience-barnsley.com/our-archives/collections** that has the catalogues, indexes and guides for various subject areas. There are downloadable guides to school records and parish councils – with the former subject to a closure period of between 50 and 100 years due to data protection. Experience Barnsley **www.experience-barnsley.com/our-archives** is the home page for Barnsley Archives and Local Studies and this leads to some collection guides and finding aids. The organisation has entered into an agreement with Ancestry for its Nonconformist registers to be digitised and made accessible online. This is due to be happening by late 2024 and is its first venture into working with a commercial family history site.

Explore centuries of history of Barnsley and surrounds at Barnsley Archives.

Doncaster

With a welcome reopening at a bespoke collections and research facility, Doncaster Archives is home to archival collections featuring historical documents dating back to the eleventh century. The archives include newspapers, maps and photos on topics including law, healthcare, education and politics. Archive material is in the process of being digitised and the online catalogue can be found at **https://library.doncaster.gov.uk/web/arena/archives**. There is also a family and local history alphabet page **https://library.doncaster.gov.uk/web/arena/archives1** with background information on the collections and links for a variety of topics.

Rotherham
Visit the Rotherham Archives and Local Studies website **www.rotherham.gov.uk/leisure-culture/archives-local-history/1** for details of archive material that dates as far back as 1328. The online catalogue **http://archives.rotherham.gov.uk/calmview/** follows the usual format, with advanced search and thumbnail images of some collection items. The organisation has also worked with Findmypast to digitise its school admission registers and log books, and offers free access to both Ancestry and Findmypast from its premises. As with most other such record offices, a paid-for research service is also available.

Sheffield
The family history page for Sheffield City Archives and Local History Library **www.sheffield.gov.uk/libraries-archives/access-archives-local-studies-library** has an A to Z of the collections and a dedicated family history page, which contains downloadable research guides. Anyone with Sheffield ancestors should visit Picture Sheffield **www.picturesheffield.com** with its thousands of searchable historical photos. New material is added to the site at a rate of around 5,000 items per year.

West Yorkshire

The West Yorkshire Archive Service (WYAS) has five offices located in Bradford, Calderdale, Kirklees, Leeds and Wakefield, with the latter holding a large number of county archives as well as archive material for the city of Wakefield. As one of the largest archives outside of London, WYAS have been serving family historians for generations. Each of these offices has its own website accessed from the hub page at **www.wyjs.org.uk/archive-service/contact-us-and-opening-times/**

The WYAS website **www.wyjs.org.uk/archive-service/** is home to a substantial online catalogue of more than 900,000 entries **www.catalogue.wyjs.org.uk/CalmView/advanced.aspx?src=CalmView.Catalog** as well as a number of guides and resources to assist researchers on various collections and resources that are held at the archives **www.wyjs.org.uk/archive-service/our-collections/guides-to-our-collections/**. Although the catalogue is not an online archive, there are a small number of images of archives available within the catalogue, such as the diaries of Yorkshire diarist Anne Lister which WYAS are in the process of decoding and transcribing with the invaluable help of remote volunteers from across the world.

A large amount of material from WYAS is available on Ancestry, including parish registers (baptism registers to 1910, marriage registers to 1935 and burials to 1985). An older site, Treasures of the West Yorkshire Archive Service **http://wyorksarchivestreasures.weebly.com/results.html,** remains a good introduction to key records.

County-wide

Borthwick Institute for Archives
One of the largest archives outside London, the Borthwick Institute for Archives has been established for more than seventy years. Online resources have their own page on the website **www.york.ac.uk/borthwick/resources/** and comprise four main collections: The Retreat Archive; Archbishops' Registers; York Cause Papers; and the Lascelles Barbados Papers.

Yorkshire Archaeological and Historical Society and Yorkshire Roots
Established in 1863, Yorkshire Archaeological and Historical Society (YAHS) promotes the study of the archaeology, history and people of the three Ridings of the historical county. The website **www.yas.org.uk** is a useful port of call for research, and membership gives you a copy of the society's occasional newsletter, thrice-yearly issues of the journal, and access to the society's library at the University of Leeds Library, as well as the wider holdings of Leeds University Library. The family section of the sites **www.yas.org.uk/Sections/Family-History/Family-history** is publicly accessible and links through to sister site Yorkshire Roots **www.yorkshireroots.org.uk** the society's online home.

Before exploring Yorkshire Roots, take time to browse the main site for its online lecture programme, book reviews and useful links page. From here, you can also access a range of useful society publications which are freely accessible at Internet Archive. There are more than 220 resources, from 1885 onwards, and many of these are the culmination of years of study, such as the Wakefield Court Rolls – chronicling an almost unbroken sequence of rolls that span six centuries. These provided a formal record of the transfer of land ownership and interestingly, the opening chapter notes that in cases where a wife was party to a land transfer, she was interviewed separately to her husband by the steward or his deputy, to ensure she had no objection to the transaction.

These rolls are not only a name-rich source of study, they also give us an insight into local topography and even neighbourhood disputes. In the introduction to volume five, we are transported back to life in seventeenth-century West Yorkshire:

Three cases of industrial pollution were recorded, or rather objections to them. John Watson, pipemaker, had been presented at the Halifax court leet in April 1664 for smoke abatement from his furnace erected at the back of his house in Halifax. He denied the charge as was brought for trial at the October court leet when the local jurors confirmed that the pipe furnace was a 'common annoyance to the neighbours' and Watson was fined £10. Sarah Baker and Mary Longbothome were presented in October 1664 for defiling the town well, the second 'sinding and washing yarn therein'. The fine in both cases was 10s. Widow Hardie was washing offal in the town well and was duly presented at the April court and fined a total of £1 for several such offences.

Yorkshire Roots also has a list of YAHS archives now in the University Library's Special Collections that can be searched online **https://library.leeds.ac.uk/special-collections/collection/1176** as well as an indexed list of names from back issues of the society's journal, and details ongoing projects.

Gateway Websites

Ancestor Search
www.ancestor-search.info/LOC-INDEX.htm is the perfect site to bookmark as it leads you down so many other pathways. Courses, talks, internet sources, subscription sites and even CDs are covered, as well as links to record office and family history society websites. Do bear in mind, however, that the site was last updated in 2017 and so you may come across some broken links.

Archives Hub
www.archiveshub.ac.uk can be used to find unique digital resources from more than 380 UK institutions, including archives, libraries museums and universities.

British History Online
A collection of thousands of volumes and images, comprising both primary and secondary source material and covering all of the UK. Whilst premium content is available by subscription, there is also plenty to explore as a free-of-charge user. The subject guides **www.british-history.ac.uk/using-bho/subject-guides** are a good place to start as each has been written by a specialist historian and gives a good overview

of each of these broad topics. From there, you can either browse the catalogue or try a keyword search.

Cyndi's List
www.cyndislist.com
This site is used the world over and, unlike some of the older gateway sites, even though this one was established twenty-five years ago, it is still regularly updated. With a massive 300,000+ links it can be hard to know where to start, but using the card catalogue can be better than just diving into a general search.

Genuki (UK and Ireland Genealogy)
The website has its own Yorkshire hub page **www.genuki.org.uk/big/eng/YKS** which itself leads to 250,000 pages of links and photographs relating to the county. Where to start? The hub page is well organised into topics and so it's really a case of what you're looking for, but the genealogy page is, of course, worth exploring. The site is strong on links for topography and place names, and has useful links to free look-up services where volunteers will help you with queries, and also has links to mailing lists and chat rooms.

UKIsearch.com
www.ukisearch.com
This is a similar project to Genuki, albeit on a smaller scale, and here you will find thousands of links to databases and record transcriptions, with 95 per cent of the resources listed being free of charge. The information is arranged by county, followed by general links, and then individual pages for towns and parishes. What you'll find here is a matter of chance; some places have several link categories, whilst others are represented only by a single link. It's well worth exploring, though, as some of the information could be difficult to track down elsewhere, such as Quaker intentions of marriage 1680–1802 for Midhope, list of Leeds Chartist candidates (1839–52) and other miscellaneous gems such as a collection of monumental inscriptions for Easingwold, the originals of which are now indecipherable.

Yorkshire Historical Dictionary
https://yorkshiredictionary.york.ac.uk
This is a large database of Yorkshire dialect words that can be a big help when transcribing old documents, or if you come across an unfamiliar term during your research. Around 4,000 words are included, spanning

the years 1100 to *c*.1750; these were collected by the late Dr George Redmonds, a name studies historian, in the course of his sixty-year career. The terms include by-names and place names; agricultural, industrial and coal-mining terms; words for landscape features, animals and plants; and the names of domestic objects, clothing and textiles. The dictionary is a growing resource, with researchers welcome to submit their own word suggestions via the 'submissions' form on the site.

Commercial Subscription Sites

All of the main commercial vendors (Ancestry, FamilySearch, Findmypast and TheGenealogist) have Yorkshire-focused collections, most of which have been made available thanks to the work of archives, libraries and volunteers across the counties over many years. Each of the sites mentioned below – with the exception of FamilySearch, which is free – makes its data available on a pay-per-view and/or subscription basis, and many offer an initial free trial for a number of days – do make sure you cancel in time if you don't wish to continue.

Save money!
Check with your local or county library if you have a library or membership card, as many offer online access to the above as part of your library membership, either at the library and/or in your own home as well as things such as the Access to Research database with millions of research articles – you can simply log in with your library account.

We'll be exploring each of these sites in more detail as we go through the coming chapters, looking at how the collections can help us with birth, marriage and death information, occupations, religion, schooldays and much more. With each of the sites, it's usually worth using the card catalogue, or at least the advanced search, as a general search from the home page will usually give you an overwhelming number of results and enough mis-matches to confuse even the keenest researcher.

Ancestry (£)
The Ancestry Yorkshire page **www.ancestry.co.uk/search/places/united_kingdom/england/yorkshire/** is the entry point for census, electoral rolls, baptism, marriage and burial, military, immigration, emigration

and lots more. A couple of collections are free to access: West Yorkshire militia 1779–1826, and quarter session records for 1637–1914.

I find Ancestry to be strongest for its West Yorkshire collections in terms of the county as a whole. For example, it has baptisms, marriages and burials from 1512 through to the twentieth century from WYAS Wakefield, plus Nonconformist records from the 1600s to 1980s. And as we'll see in later chapters, you can also explore West Yorkshire records such as electoral registers, prison records and tax valuations.

FamilySearch
The world's largest online genealogy site has plenty of Yorkshire material and we have some expert tips on negotiating the birth, marriage and burial records in Chapter 2. Start on the FamilySearch Wiki **www.familysearch.org/en/wiki/Yorkshire,_England_Genealogy** for links through to resources and help pages, plus lists of Yorkshire parishes and civil districts.

Another helpful page is **www.familysearch.org/en/wiki/Yorkshire_Archives_and_Libraries** for links to dozens of libraries and archives. Steven Archer, creator of the surname distribution map (available from his site on CD), has created a helpful guide to British batches **www.archersoftware.co.uk/igi/index.htm** that you can use to make your searches on the site more powerful. This is a complicated topic but very simply, searches on FamilySearch allow you to use surname only if you are searching a specific set of records, rather than on the whole site. So, if you have the batch number for a record set, your searches should be much more fruitful. For more background on this, see **https://freepages.rootsweb.com/~hughwallis/genealogy/IGIBatchNumbers.htm**.

Using FamilySearch: expert tips
Steven Bruce of Yorkshire Family History **www.yorkshirefamilyhistory.org** (see also Chapter 9), explains just why he finds the world's largest family history website so useful:

Most researchers, including those who are new to researching their ancestry, will already have become familiar with the records currently available via the online services of Ancestry, Findmypast, TheGenealogist et al. These services have evolved over the last twenty years or so and are now considered to be the main 'go to' websites for genealogical content to include the main classes of record such as census returns, parish registers and non-parochial records. These websites provide a relatively straightforward means by which to search for your ancestors.

However, the forerunner of all the above-mentioned genealogical content providers, and many others, is FamilySearch. For experienced family historians, FamilySearch remains the colossus. For example, in terms of the amount of genealogical data that is available on the FamilySearch website, a note on their Explore Historical Images section of the site states, 'Search groups of images in the world's largest collection of historical documents, with over 4,988,112,965 images and counting'. On the front page of the above-mentioned section of the website, that astonishing figure can be seen increasing in front of your eyes and is fast approaching 5,000 million ... this is most definitely the world's largest collection of historical documents.

So, whilst the Internet is now awash with some extremely useful content, which is being provided by a plethora of content providers enabling us to assemble a family tree that records the vital information of our ancestors, there is also a wealth of family history data available which lies beyond this vital information. FamilySearch is just one such avenue that can be pursued.

It is a fact that the genealogy of our ancestors is required before we can start to clothe this information with family history. Which means that the vital details of an individual are required so that connections can be made to other generations up and down the ancestral family line. In other words, evidence of birth, baptism, marriage, death and burial, along with perhaps the occupation of an individual and whether they made a will which was proved in a court of probate forms the corner stone of our research. However, simply searching for these vital details of an individual is only the start of the genealogical journey. It is the continuing research beyond finding these vital details of our ancestors, which makes us family historians.

Due to the ever-presence of some of the commercial genealogical content providers, it would be easy for a newcomer to genealogical research to overlook the FamilySearch website, and if the FamilySearch website is overlooked, the Explore Historical Images pages of the website would also be overlooked.

Successful genealogical and family history research is all about 'knowing what is available and knowing where to find it'. My top tip, although I should say that I can readily think of many other top tips that could be vying for the top slot, is the Explore Historical Images section of the FamilySearch website, which can be located at **www.familysearch.org/records/images/**.

The front page of this section invites you to enter the name of a parish, city, town or village, so just type in the places in which you have an interest. If say, you entered York, and then from the drop-down choice, choose York, Yorkshire, England, United Kingdom, 1801-Present – Town, and then press the Search Image Groups button, you will be offered (at the time of writing) 487 image collections of City of York records to include:

Military Records, Militia Records, Voting Registers, Court Records, Guild Records, Occupation Records, Rate Books, Business Records, Residence Records, Vaccination Registers, Overseers Records, Will Records, Cemetery Records, Cemetery Indexes, Estate Records, Land Records, Apprenticeship Indentures, Settlement Records, Bastardy Bonds, Parish Poor Law Records, Freeman of the City Records, Hearth Tax Records, Window Tax Records, etc.

All these images, amounting to a few hundred thousand, are usually digitised images of the microfilm version of original documents currently held at the City of York Archives, and ALL this digitised data is free to view, no subscription required.

Just type in your place(s) of interest to find your own family history nuggets.

Findmypast (£)
The site's Yorkshire page **www.Findmypast.co.uk/articles/world-records/search-all-uk-records/special-collections/the-yorkshire-collection** includes the records of six Yorkshire archives who have provided source material dating back to the sixteenth century. Findmypast has a good parish record collection and unique material such as a rare surviving 1831 census for Nether Hallam township in Sheffield. Speaking of Sheffield, some of the site's holdings relating to the city aren't listed under Yorkshire categories, so always include 'Sheffield' in your searches if it's of interest.

Just as Ancestry is strong on West Yorkshire material, Findmypast holdings include records from the archives of Doncaster, Sheffield, Teesside, East Riding, and North Yorkshire County Record Office. It also holds valuable information from the National Will Index, including the

York Peculiars probate collection for 1383 to 1883 and the York medieval probate index covering 1267 to 1500.

One of the most recent additions is the Sheffield Archives and Local Studies Composite Personal Name Index, a database of 260,000 names from various records including: Ecclesall Bierlow workhouse registers of inmates, quarter sessions prison calendars, magistrates' court records, police charge books, South Yorkshire asylum admission registers, House of Help case books, etc.).

MyHeritage (£)
The Yorkshire collections at MyHeritage can be accessed at the card catalogue **www.myheritage.com/records/United-Kingdom/all-records?q= Yorkshire** with twenty-six collections to explore, including several old books.

TheGenealogist (£)
Master Search at TheGenealogist **www.thegenealogist.co.uk/search/ master/** allows you to locate its Yorkshire records, including reference books, tithe maps and the census.

Free BMD/FreeCen/FreeReg
This free-to-use group of sites is the home of an ongoing project to transcribe family history records and allow people around the world to access this information free of charge. Each of these sites is a work in progress as volunteers add new records to the site and so they are well worth bookmarking to return to periodically.

Free BMD provides free online access to the GRO Index, transcribing the civil registration index of births, marriages and deaths **www.freebmd. org.uk**. At FreeCen **www.freecen.org.uk** you can search nineteenth-century census returns (again, a work in progress, and with FreeReg, explore baptism, marriage and burial records from 1538 onwards, from church records: **www.freereg.org.uk**.

Yorkshire-specific Websites
This final section introduces a number of Yorkshire-specific sites that can help once you've established the basic facts on your family tree. Again, these are the result of years of work from dedicated family historians, some of whom have provided the expert tips in this and later chapters.

Dave King Genealogy

www.davekinggenealogy.co.uk is the online home of several useful and name-rich projects. Among the gems are extracts of personal names from wills proved in the Durham registry and the Prerogative Court of Canterbury (PCC) (which covers Cleveland areas of North Yorkshire), and also wills proved the exchequer and prerogative courts at York.

The Denby Dale & Kirkburton Online Archive Collection

www.denbydalekirkburtonarchives.co.uk celebrates the rich heritage of the Denby Dale and Kirkburton areas of West Yorkshire and includes digital images of a wide range of original archives from a range of sources. From the collections of WYAS, the website includes records (mostly meeting minutes) of the townships, local boards and urban district councils of Denby Dale, Clayton West, Cumberworth, Emley and Skelmanthorpe areas, from the late nineteenth century to the 1970s. The original archives are still held by West Yorkshire Archive Service Kirklees (at Halifax).

Medieval genealogy

www.medievalgenealogy.org.uk is a useful, name-rich resource for those long-ago ancestors who can be difficult to find via the subscription sites. For example, the Tempest family study **www.medievalgenealogy.org.uk/families/tempest/index.shtml** has genealogical studies of the Yorkshire Tempest family, and a researched pedigree. The site also has useful guides on carrying out medieval genealogy research, including guidance on topics such as heraldry and manorial records.

Steve Whitwam's Family History Site

www.whitwam.co.uk/index.htm is full of useful resources for Colne Valley (West Yorkshire) ancestors. He was one of the people who helped set up Huddersfield Family History Society and since then has been responsible for creating a large number of online resources, including census indexes. Steve offers free advice and lookups for anyone with Colne Valley connections, a helpful service that has proved to be of assistance to his own research, since many local families will be connected; as a result, he has made contacts with people in the US, Australia, Canada and Greece.

Chapter 2

VITAL RECORDS FOR BIRTH, MARRIAGE AND DEATH

In this chapter, we take a look at the vital records that record the birth (and/or baptism), marriage and death (and/or burial) of our ancestors. It is through this information that we can not only find out when our ancestor lived and how long their life was, but these records are also our key to discovering the next generation back in time, as many will include the name of a person's parents and even grandparents.

We have three key topics in this chapter: records of birth, marriage and death in the years following civil registration in 1837; parish registers for pre-civil registration events; and the many other records that can help us to explore the birth, marriage and death of our ancestors alongside the three key record sets. As we'll discover, when researching Yorkshire ancestors, we have access to a very special record set that is (almost) unique to the county, and can give us up to four generations of a family in one record.

Part 1 – Post-1837: Civil Registration

Because it's best to start with yourself and work backwards when tracing your family tree, we'll begin with the most recent record sets available to us: the records of civil registration. These are official, national records of the birth, marriage and death of every individual in England and they have been kept since 1 July 1837, when the Births and Deaths Registration Act came into being – although it was not actually compulsory to register births until 1874.

In order to find out more information about an ancestor's birth, marriage or death, you will need to send for the relevant certificate from the General Record Office (GRO). Many years ago, this would have involved a physical trip to the search through the GRO index books, but now these indexes are available online and it is the information within these that you'll need in order to send for the correct document – for each certificate you send for, you'll be asked for the volume number and page number, to make sure that the correct record is retrieved.

Yorkshire Birth, Marriages and Deaths
www.yorkshirebmd.org.uk is part of the wider Local BMD Project. Here, you can freely explore indexes of birth, marriages and deaths across the county from the start of civil registration in 1837. At the time of writing there were 3.5 million births, 1.3million marriages and 1.4 million death indexes. The database is still growing and so if you don't find what you're looking for the first time, bookmark the site for later use. You can find tutorials on how to get the best from the sites at the home hub **www.ukbmd.org.uk/tutorials**. The site is now in its third decade and is supported by a range of libraries, archives and societies.

The indexes are also available at commercial providers Ancestry (transcribed by FreeBMD) Findmypast, MyHeritage and TheGenealogist, and the GRO also has its own index. Steven Bruce of Yorkshire Family History suggests the GRO website for searching for births in particular, remarking that the inclusion of the mother's maiden surname in the birth indexes back to 1837 has reopened one or two of his past cases.

> **Save money!**
> Whichever way you find your volume and page numbers, it's advisable to send for the certificate from the GRO itself, as prices can be higher if you go via third-party websites.

What information can be found on a birth certificate?
- Name of the child
- Date of birth
- Place of birth
- Father's name and occupation
- Mother's name and maiden name

What information can be found on a marriage certificate?
- First name and surname of the bride and groom
- Marriage date
- Marital status
- Age of bride and groom

- Occupation
- Fathers' names (bride and groom)
- Residence at the time of marriage
- Names of witnesses

What information can be found on a death certificate?
- Date of death
- Full name
- Age
- Occupation
- Cause of death
- Description and residence of informant
- When the death was registered

Part 2 – Pre-1837: Parish Registers

It's important to remember that no one website has all of the parish records – and indeed, a good many of these records are not available online, and yet more have been lost forever, due to fire, flood, war and so on.

Until the mid-nineteenth century, the vast majority of baptisms, marriages and burials were carried out by the Church of England. Bear in mind that these are records of baptism and not birth – there could have been months or even years between a birth and a baptism, and they are records of burial and not death – in this case the gap between the two will generally be shorter than it might be between a birth and baptism.

The majority of England's parish registers from 1538 onwards have been deposited at the relevant county record office; very few are still held by the church where the event was registered. The online catalogue of each record office will list what parish registers are held, the dates covered, any missing registers and also whether – and where – these can be accessed online. Particularly during the Civil War period of 1642–51, many registers were lost or were not kept at all.

Entrance to Ledsham parish church, West Yorkshire. As one of England's oldest parish churches, it has both surviving Saxon and Norman features. (© Storye Book)

When using websites to access these records, what you are using are indexed digital images. As you go further back in time you will encounter the use of Latin as this was England's official written language until 1733 – although many records were written in English before this. The prospect of using Latin records may seem a little daunting, but knowing a few key terms – such as *filius* for son and *filia* for daughter, *uxoris* for wife, and *sepult* or *sep* for burial, should allow you to proceed with just a little detective work.

> **Latin in parish records**
> Genuki has an expert guide to the Latin terms you're likely to come across whilst exploring parish records. Visit **www.genuki.org.uk/big/LatinNotes**.

When searching online, you may come across the term bishops' registers or transcripts. These began in 1597 and are essentially an extra copy of the original records kept by a parish church and will contain similar, if not exactly the same, information. They can be extremely useful should the original records have been lost or destroyed and, in some cases, are the only record of a baptism, marriage or burial having taken place.

So how do you bridge the gap between finding an ancestor in post-1837 records and going back into parish records from before the start of civil registration? Here, the census is your guide. Any UK census from 1851 onwards will give your ancestor's age and place of birth, allowing you to find out where and in what year to start your search of the parish registers. Although the 1841 census doesn't give place of birth and only has approximate age, you can still use it to see who your ancestor was living with and where, again to help you decide where to focus your search.

Finding Records for Your Parish of Interest

Yorkshire Parish Registers
https://yorkshireparishregisters.com/about-us-1-w.asp is a site that makes available the work of The Yorkshire Parish Register Society, which between 1899 and 2014 transcribed and published volumes of original parish registers. Almost all the volumes contain indexes to surnames, Christian names, places and occupations. From the 1950s onwards, the volumes have included extra material to be found in the Bishop's Transcripts, especially useful where parts of the original registers are

deficient. The volumes are sold as CDs, books and downloads and you can see a list of parishes covered on the home page.

For the best chance of finding a particular ancestor when researching in the era of parish records, you need to work out in which parish the life event is likely to have occurred. Although some villages and small towns may only have had one parish church, as the population boomed and became more urbanised in the nineteenth century, one city could contain many parishes. FamilySearch is a great help here, with historical maps, parish information and dates: see the parishes section at **www.familysearch.org/en/wiki/Yorkshire,_England_Genealogy** then click on your parish of interest for its history, neighbouring parishes and location of church records. There is a table for online records which covers baptism, marriage and burial, and the years covered; Genuki also has similar information.

You can find volumes of transcribed parish registers covering centuries at Internet Archive **https://archive.org/search.php?query=parish%20registers%20yorkshire** where you can also read the seminal text *Parish Registers of England* by John Charles Cox.

It's important to be aware that, unlike the GRO records, there is no central location – online or offline – for parish registers. Most are kept at county record offices and by no means all have been digitised. This

East Witton parish church. When searching for an ancestor's baptism, marriage or burial record, it's important to try to establish the parish they were based in. (© Kreuzschnabel, CCASA, 3.0)

is crucial to bear in mind if you're struggling to find a particular birth, marriage or death via an online search – that record may well exist but not have been digitised. Having said that, more material is put online every year, for example North Yorkshire County Record Office recently added their parish registers to Ancestry.

Dade Parish Registers
Before delving into the sections of parish registers of birth, marriage and burial, this is a good time to introduce a hugely useful type of register that is almost unique to Yorkshire – the Dade parish registers.

If you've traced your ancestors back beyond the start of civil registration in 1837, chances are you might have heard of the Dade registers, or perhaps even come across one such record – and been impressed at its wealth of detail – but not actually realised what it was.

Discovering English Ancestors **http://englishancestors.byu.edu/Pages/dade-registers** is the online home of these records (now also available on Ancestry and Findmypast as part of their parish registers collections) and the site hosts the only digital catalogue and map of parishes the records cover. The registers are named after eighteenth-century Yorkshire clergyman William Dade who, along with several other men of his profession, took it upon himself to add extra information to the standard details given on baptism, marriage and burial records. So, if you're lucky enough to see an ancestor featured, not only might you find out about the new baby's parents, you could add an extra generation, as grandparents are included too, as well as details such as abode and occupation. For burials you could be lucky enough to find a parent listed even for a person who died in their nineties. Clearly, in an era before central records such as the census and civil registration, these details could be invaluable, particularly if you're unsure which ancestor is yours from a group of several potential candidates.

The Discovering English Ancestors website described above lists all of the parishes that have any Dade registers and these are also shown on a map, together with details of the years covered and what extra information was given. You can also download the data as an Excel spreadsheet. Because most of the parishes that adopted Dade's scheme were within a few miles of York, most of the resulting records (the core years of the scheme were 1777 to 1812) are at The Borthwick, University of York. Finding these records is a little hit and miss since there is no central holding point; you may just happen to stumble upon a record during the course of your research. Historian Roger Bellingham has a useful guide at **https://bit.ly/3odCzZ0**.

> **What might you discover?**
> With several John and Stephen Crofts in her family tree, fellow genealogist Gaynor Haliday was not only able to find the right family line through the Dade registers for Bolton Abbey but also occupations, addresses and a couple of astonishing facts.
>
> The baptism of her known 4 x great grandfather John Croft on 4 August 1799 listed his father (Stephen, butcher, Halton), his grandparents (John Croft, stuff weaver, Jubiler, Beamsley, and Elizabeth Brigg) his great grandparents (Stephen Brigg and Margaret Dawson) 2 x great grandparents (James Dawson and Margaret Benson) and a 3 x great grandfather (Charles Benson of Halton).
>
> Earlier parish records, though not as detailed, showed Stephen Brigg (1718–1781) as the son of Stephen Brigg (a yeoman) and Elinor Petyt. Stephen Brigg senior was born in 1679 and died 30 January 1782! His gravestone records him slightly erroneously as being 105, but the burial records have it right as 103. Elinor was the 2 x great granddaughter of Anthonie Petyt, the uncle of William and Sylvester, both born at a humble farm in Storiths, near Bolton Abbey in the late 1630s. William became the keeper of the records in the Tower of London, while Sylvester pursued a legal career. Both were major benefactors to Ermysted's Grammar School in Skipton where they'd been educated, with Sylvester leaving an incredible £30,000 to the school on his death in 1719. These brothers are Gaynor's first cousins twelve times removed! And their birthplace still stands.

Birth/baptism records

Baptism records in the parish registers will give you information on the person (usually a baby or child) being baptised, plus the name of the father and sometimes the mother. However, unlike with more modern birth certificates, the mother's maiden name will not be given, if she is mentioned at all. Remember that the date of baptism is not the date of birth, although this date may occasionally be recorded. Be aware of children from the same family being baptised in 'batches' – seeing two or more children baptised on the same day in one family doesn't necessarily mean you've stumbled upon twins or triplets.

Bear in mind also that particularly before the twentieth century, many couples didn't marry until after the birth of one or more children, or perhaps tied the knot whilst the bride was pregnant.

> **Tantalising clues in the registers**
> The beauty of parish registers is that unlike their regimented post-1837 counterparts, they can provide tantalising clues about an ancestor's circumstances because of the scope that the vicar had when completing the register.
>
> For example, the baptism record of my ancestor James Holroyd in Pontefract in September 1815 provided me with a valuable clue about his father. Although James's father (also named James) was deceased at the time of the baptism, the vicar has helpfully recorded that James senior had been a corporal of the 33rd Foot who was killed at the Battle of Waterloo three months earlier. I was then able to follow the trail and find out more about James senior's experiences in the battle, including the number of casualties, the uniform, and the role that his regiment played in the engagement: **www.dwr.org.uk/history/regimental-battle-honours/quatre-bras-waterloo-1815/**.

Marriage records

Marriage records are one of the stepping stones of family history, as it is here that you will discover the maiden name of your ancestor's mother, and thus add not only another generation to your tree, but another surname to research. From 1832 onwards, a marriage record will give you the age, occupation and father's name for both bride and groom.

As with baptisms, all of the major commercial genealogy websites have marriage indexes for pre-1837 unions. The information you find may vary and you are also likely to come across banns, which contain similar information to a record of marriage, and in some cases, might be the only surviving record of the union (although of course the fact that banns were called is not absolute proof that the marriage did go ahead. Banns were the public announcement of an intention to marry, in order to give notice to anyone who wished to object to the marriage on legal or canonical grounds.) Both banns and marriage records may contain the bride and groom's home parish, as well as the parish where the marriage was to take place – usually the home parish of the bride or groom.

The year 1812 is a landmark one for marriage records, since before this date you may find that just the name of the bride and groom were recorded in the parish register. After 1812, ministers also had to declare the marital status of each (e.g. spinster, widow), parish and age – sometimes recorded simply as 'of full age', which means over 21. After this date you should also find the signature or 'x' mark of the couple, as well as details of witnesses.

Joiner Marriage Index
The Joiner Marriage Index (£) **http://joinermarriageindex.co.uk** is run by Paul Joiner (see tip below) and has more than 3 million hand-verified marriage records from over 5,000 parishes in 38 English and Welsh counties. These are pre-1837 records which you can search for free and then pay for further details once you've identified the correct record. This resource is an index of the marriage records from parish registers, not actual marriage certificates. The cost of a search begins at £2.29 for a single marriage record and increases by £0.10 per marriage record up to a maximum of £52.19 for 500 marriage records. If you do make a payment, be aware that once payment has been made you must wait to be returned to the site. Pressing the back button causes a fault and the results will not appear even though payment has been taken. (The site team can spot that this has happened and can manually make the search, but it is preferable if things work automatically.)

> **Expert tip**
> Paul Joiner of Joiner Marriage Index advises: 'When using Joiner Marriage Index, consider using our alternative search modes, Soundex and Metaphone. We consider they are better when one notes the variability of surname spelling in the past. Of the two, Soundex is somewhat better known but we find Metaphone to be even better.'

As well as giving you information about the fathers of the bride and groom, you will also have the names of two witnesses to the marriage and these are always worth investigating, as many turn out either to be family members or close friends, either of which could turn up again in your research at a later date, perhaps as the beneficiary of a bequest or the witness to a will, or as a household member in a later census, perhaps. Although the printed registers provide two spaces for witnesses, there are very often many more people listed.

The place of the marriage is also worth exploring, not only to look at the history of the church in which the ceremony took place (for example, are other family members buried in the churchyard, does the church still exist?) but also because this may give you a clue as to the place of birth for either or both the bride or bridegroom. Alternatively, if any prior or subsequent children's births took place in different parishes, this may indicate that the family was moving around regularly, perhaps for work reasons.

Burial records

It can be tempting to dismiss burial records as less important than records of birth and marriage, but these too can help us to find out more information about the final years of our ancestors, and introduce new family members to our tree.

As mentioned earlier, this particular type of parish register relates to the date of burial not of death, although date of death may be mentioned on the record – or you may discover it from probate records. You may also encounter some inaccuracy with regard to age, as those giving and recording the information may not have been sure of the exact date – or even year – of birth of the deceased.

Newspaper obituaries can also be a valuable source of clues, giving you information such as burial place, funeral details and the names of relatives. If you can't find the record of a death, go back through the censuses until you find the final one that mentions your ancestor and use this record to get the person's last address and then try to work back from there. Even occupation could be a clue if the person wasn't retired.

You can explore burial records at the main genealogy websites, for example TheGenealogist has parish registers for more than 100 parishes at **www.thegenealogist.co.uk/coverage/parish-records/yorkshire/** and here you can look up your parish in the alphabetical list and see which years are covered; some start as early as the fifteenth century. For example, Kirk Ella, to the west of Hull in East Yorkshire has burial records at TheGenealogist from 1441 through to 1837, although there are gaps of quite a few years during this long run. This is a fact that's helpful to note before you begin your search since you may be able to track down the missing years on other sites, or discover that the records for that particular year have been lost.

Whether or not you're able to discover a burial record, you can complete the circle of life by attempting to find your ancestor's final resting place and there are several means of doing this online. As we shall see, a gravestone usually has extra information, and if you're actually able to visit the site, or even browse the burial records online, you might also find other family members buried nearby.

So, how to go about this? For pre-1837 burials you will usually be looking at burial in the churchyard of your ancestor's parish church, in a plot that may or may not still exist. After the start of civil registration, and the growth in population that accompanied the Industrial Revolution, we start to see our ancestors being buried in cemeteries that may not have been attached to a parish church.

To find where the dates and location of burial records of your parish of interest, start in the parishes collection of the Yorkshire Genealogy section of FamilySearch **www.familysearch.org/en/wiki/Yorkshire_ Parishes_A-I** and scroll down to the coloured table. This diagram is divided into birth, marriage and death records, and gives you the relevant dates and one or more websites that hold this information. For example, for Keighley in West Yorkshire, you can explore burial records covering the period from the 1500s to the 1900s at six different websites and for non-C of E, Keighley researchers are referred to the Nonconformist records at Findmypast.

The engraving on a gravestone is called a monumental inscription (MI) and these are your online gateway to accessing details about an ancestor's gravestone if you can't visit in person, if the engraving has become illegible over the centuries, or if the burial plot or the whole burial ground no longer exist. Here, we owe a debt of gratitude to volunteers across the county who have carried out recording projects, either independently or as part of a heritage or family history society, and those who have subsequently uploaded and published this data.

Family history societies are a first port of call for MIs and all you have to do here is to identify your parish of interest and then visit the site of the society in question; any monumental inscription projects should be listed either in the 'project' or 'publications' section or of course, you can ask. The data is usually available on a CD or database and typically would be in alphabetical order by name, so that if you know your ancestor's approximate date of death you should be able to identify them. Societies such as East Yorkshire Family History Society **www.eyfhs.org.uk/monumental-inscriptions** have published MI books or CDs of inscriptions in various churchyards. If you know that an ancestor was, or may have been, buried there, you can send for the relevant MI publication or access it online. This is particularly helpful if you're unable to visit the burial ground, or if the inscriptions have deteriorated and are no longer readable. Projects such as these are a real labour of love, as volunteers will have spent hours scouring burial grounds in all weathers, contending with overgrown plants, precariously balanced monuments and of course, the British weather.

Findmypast has a MI collection at **https://search.Findmypast.co.uk/ search-world-records/yorkshire-monumental-inscriptions** provided in partnership with family history societies and the Family History Federation. See the parish list at **www.Findmypast.co.uk/articles/ yorkshire-monumental-inscriptions-parish-lists** for the different areas covered.

You can also explore for free at UK BMD www.ukbmd.org.uk/county/yorkshire/monumental_inscriptions/, FamilySearch https://bit.ly/42cslbb and Yorkshire Burials – the latter is definitely worth bookmarking for its focus on the county.

Yorkshire Burials **https://yorkshireburials.uk** is a free database of burial records, monumental inscriptions and plans which began as a Leeds-focused project and over the years, has grown to encompass the whole county. At the time of writing, the site has records of more than 900,000 burials across municipal, parish and Nonconformist burial grounds, with information from over 340,000 parish burials. After creating a free account, you can search by a number of filters including name, burial ground, year of birth, area and cemetery name. If you strike lucky, the individual records can give really useful information such as last address, name of relatives such as parents, spouse, children etc., age at death and even burial number, the latter useful should you wish to try to see the plot for yourself. The 'persons in the grave' section on some of the individual entries shows who else is buried in the same plot, potentially giving you a set of ancestors at one click.

The main focus of the site over the past few years has been the transcript of some of the Yorkshire Archaeological Society (YAS) records, which were 18,000 pages of mainly handwritten documents collected by the YAS over a long period. You can see the progress so far on at the Yorkshire Burials website under 'YAS Project'. The team are also involved

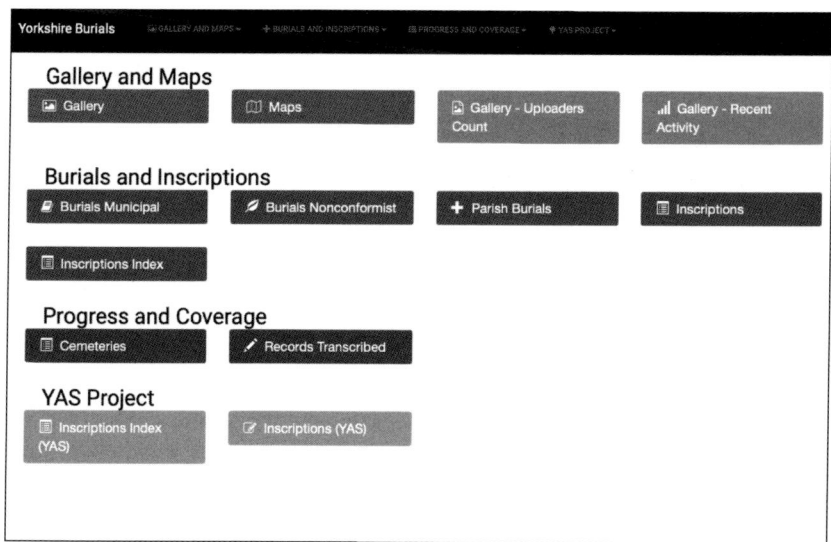

Yorkshire burials covers more than 800,000 municipal cemeteries across the county.

in photographing and transcribing headstones throughout Yorkshire and in their gallery section, you can see that over 100,000 have been completed so far. Volunteers are also undertaking geolocating graves in the larger cemeteries to assist people in finding the headstones and also transcribe parish and municipal burial records, with over a million records now on the website.

The Leeds Municipal Cemeteries' project is the biggest project on the website, covering all records held by the Leeds Bereavement Services, who granted Yorkshire Burials access to the original burial registers when they were based at Lawnswood. This includes access to the grave books and plans. The project was originally called Leeds Burials RIP (records, inscriptions and plans). The records were not available on the large genealogy sites and so it became a unique online reference for people searching for burials in the Leeds area. In addition, and with the permission of the Leeds University, Woodhouse General Cemetery was transcribed and added to the collection. As were, with permission from the Leeds Diocese, the burial records for the Leeds Catholic Cemetery based at Killingbeck.

A gravestone can tell us so much about an ancestor's life, family and beliefs. Shown here is a stone in Harlow Hill Cemetery, Harrogate. (© Linda Spashnett, CCASA 3.0)

Finally, two larger-scale sites, not Yorkshire focused but potentially useful nonetheless are FindAGrave **www.findagrave.com,** billed as the world's largest gravesite collection and internment.net **www.interment.net/Default.htm** with worldwide listings.

Part 3 – Records to Supplement Birth, Marriage and Death Records

In this section, we take a look at the records that can help us flesh out our research and bring things to life once we've explored the key record sets relating to baptism, marriage and burial.

Wills

Many of us consider records relating to death to be the least fruitful in terms of information, but wills can give us many clues not only about what our ancestor owned, but their wishes at the time the document was created and also information on extended family.

The commercial websites each have their own collection. Ancestry has indexes for records covering 1521 to 1828 – records of the former archdeaconry areas of Richmond and Knaresborough. Findmypast's holdings include a medieval probate index for York (1267–1500), which has some of England's earliest wills available online. TheGenealogist's collection of wills includes indexes of wills from the fourteenth to seventeenth centuries: Wills in the York Registry, 1603–11; Yorkshire Wills 1389–1602; Yorkshire Wills 1612–52. When you find an ancestor listed in any of the above, you can order a copy of the original record from the Borthwick Institute for Archives.

Do bear in mind that the date a will was recorded is the date it was proved, not the date it was written or the date of death. West Yorkshire Archive Service has a good collection guide at **www.wyjs.org.uk/media/1573/collection-guide-4-wills.pdf** and this includes guidance on wills held by WYAS covering both the North and East Ridings. There is also a helpful glossary for terms you may come across during your research, such as 'relict' for the person left behind after the death of a spouse, and 'codicil', which is an alteration or addition to a will.

The Borthwick Institute holds half a million wills, dating from 1267 to 1858, the majority of which are from Yorkshire: **www.york.ac.uk/borthwick/**. There are three ways in which you can search for individuals in the database of wills and administrations:

- Contact the Borthwick to request a search – staff can carry out up to five searches free of charge.
- Visit the archive in York and search the indexes for free.
- Search the indexes at Findmypast. These include wills proved in the Prerogative and Exchequer Courts of York between 1267–1501 and 1688–1858, and wills proved in the Peculiar Courts of York 1383–1833. Visit **https://search.Findmypast.co.uk/search-united-kingdom-records-in-birth-marriage-death-and-parish-records/and_wills-and-probate**.

For the Archdeaconry of Richmond (includes some parts of North Yorkshire) and Masham Peculiar, enquire at West Yorkshire Archive Service Leeds.

After 1858, wills were proved by the national Probate Registry and you can search these at **www.gov.uk/search-will-probate**.

Bastardy records
Your first indication that an ancestor was illegitimate might be if you find a birth certificate with no father listed, or a baptism record that either doesn't mention a father, or explicitly states that the child is what was at the time termed a 'baseborn child' or 'bastard'. All is not lost in term of finding the father, however, as you may either discover that the parents married soon afterwards, or that the mother was able to pursue the father through official channels in order to claim maintenance for her child. Ancestry has such records for West Yorkshire, 1690–1914, **www.ancestry.co.uk/search/collections/2582/** which are part of the WYAS Poor Law records collection and were produced either as the result of a mother pursuing a father for support, as mentioned, or when a parish attempted to hold a father responsible for a child's maintenance, and summoned the reputed father to appear in court, in order to avoid responsibility of the child falling to the parish. A bastardy order ordered the father to make payments, the bond recorded his agreement to pay, and payment registers record the father's payments.

Parish chest records
Often rich in the names of individuals, parish records can include things such as churchwarden accounts, parish apprenticeships, local tax and rate records, and church court records, as well as wills. FamilySearch has a good overview at **www.familysearch.org/en/wiki/England_Church_Records#Parish_Chest_Records**.

One good way to immerse yourself in the everyday round of parish life is through vestry minutes, which cover nominated churchwardens and the overseers of the poor, who set parish rates, oversaw the accounts and decided how parish money would be spent, for example on the highways, to support the poor of the parish, etc. These minutes may list those employed by the church to carry out repairs, such as carpenters, roofers and so on, and could list who sat in which pew of the church, bequests made, the names of poor parishioners and how long they were in receipt of aid. The overseers of the poor were tasked with collection and distributing the poor rates and for finding work and apprenticeships for the eligible poor.

Other record collections to look out for include settlement certificates, removal orders and bastardy bonds, all of which would be a treasured find if an ancestor was mentioned. For example, a settlement certificate would contain the answers a person had given about where they were born and their family circumstances. If you use parish registers in conjunction with other parish records you can find out what parish life was like and delve deep into the lives of your ancestors.

In terms of accessing these online, the main commercial websites all have their own collections, often published in conjunction with family history societies. You can also try a search with the words 'parish records' and the name of your place of interest all within quote marks. Genuki and FamilySearch also have good summaries for most Yorkshire communities.

Chapter 3

HOME LIFE: THE CENSUS AND HOUSE HISTORY

After birth, marriage and death records, the ten-yearly census is probably the most illuminating for family historians when it comes both to discerning the age, profession and whereabouts of our ancestors, and gaining a sense of the household in which they lived and who their neighbours were.

The Census

The census is truly a key family history document, allowing us to find out where our ancestors were born, lived and worked over the decades. If you have an ancestor who was born around the start of the Victorian age, you could in theory follow them through each census from childhood up until old age in 1921, which is the most recent census open to the public.

The first full census for England was taken in 1841 and with the exception of the year 1941 (due to the Second World War) has been taken every ten years since. Broadly speaking, each census asked more questions than the one that came before it, and you can find out what questions were asked at the National Archive census hub page **www.nationalarchives.gov.uk/help-with-your-research/research-guides/census-records/**.

Despite the undoubted value of the census, sadly not all of the census returns have survived, which means in some instances you may struggle to find an ancestor because their information is no longer available. You can find a summary of areas known to have missing returns at Findmypast: **www.Findmypast.co.uk/articles/census-for-england-wales-and-scotland-missing-pieces**. The prospect is also poor in terms of using the census for twentieth-century research since the 1931 census was lost in a fire, and as the 1941 was never taken, it means that the next available census (1951) will not be released until 2052. Happily, though, there are other documents that act as partial substitutes for the census, allowing us to piece together some information about more recent forebears.

England census dates
6 June 1841
30 March 1851
7 April 1861
2 April 1871
3 April 1881
5 April 1891
31 March 191
2 April 1911
19 June 1921

Online access to the census
The National Archives research guide **www.nationalarchives.gov.uk/help-with-your-research/research-guides/census-records/** has plenty of information on starting your search, what to do if you can't find an ancestor listed and how the information was taken, as well as its potential limitations.

Both Ancestry and Findmypast have images and indexes for 1841 to 1911 censuses and you can also access some of the records at FreeCen **www.freecen.org.uk**. At the time of writing, the 1921 census is available online only at Findmypast. FamilySearch has free indexes to the census returns for the 1841 to 1911 censuses. TheGenealogist also has records for every census from 1841 to 1911 and the 1939 Register.

At the Yorkshire Census website **https://yorkshirecensus.co.uk** you can access census data either on the website or as a CD-ROM for the decades covering 1841–1911. You can search the site for free, and then decide whether to pay to view the relevant record. The case studies section shows census data for textile pioneer Sir Titus Salt, and for the Brontë family of authors.

As with most other family history records, the information you can explore today can be subject to errors, and with the census there are at least two ways in which errors can creep in, potentially 'hiding' your ancestor from your searches. The information that we access nowadays was originally copied from a form completed by the census enumerator, and later by our own ancestral head of household. A small spelling mistake or even the person taking the census mishearing the information can change a forename, surname or place of birth. Since the original copies were taken, further errors may have crept in when this information was transcribed for online use. However, read on for strategies for finding 'lost' ancestors.

Before starting your search at your chosen website, it can be very useful to read the instructions that the census enumerator was given for each census. The late Guy Etchells compiled a database of this information, which you can access at Rootsweb: **https://freepages.rootsweb.com/~framland/history/census/1841directions.htm**. Looking at this data is helpful for seeing the permitted abbreviations should you come across a set of letters you don't understand. The instructions also told the enumerator what should be done in cases such as a baby not yet having been given a name, coming across an empty house, whether to record those absent from their usual place of residence, plus a myriad of other situations.

Using the census

There are many different ways to use the census apart from seeing your ancestor at ten-yearly intervals, Obviously, the information given provides certain facts – or at least, the information that was given to the enumerator. You can find out age, full name, place of birth, address, other occupants of the household and, in later censuses, occupation. If an ancestor appears to be boarding at an address, or to have boarders

Be sure to check neighbouring properties on the census, to get an idea of the relative prosperity of the street, and the various trades carried out by its occupants. (© The New York Public Library. (1814). *Wensley Dale knitters*)

in the house, it's always worth cross-checking the relevant names against your family tree, as often young or elderly relatives would stay with established families, sometimes for extended periods of time. For example, an older female relative could give you a clue as to a woman's maiden name if she turns out to be the male head of household's mother-in-law.

Bear in mind that people often gave the wrong information – deliberately or erroneously and so if you can double-check a fact elsewhere, it's wise to do so, particularly when it comes to age.

Beyond the basics, you can use census data to gain a better understanding of your ancestor's life as you follow them through the censuses. Their occupation might change and with it their social status, for better or worse. It's always interesting, too, to look at the census returns for other households in the same street or even town, to give you an understanding of the composition of the area as a whole. You may strike it lucky and find other family members living in nearby households.

You can get various printable charts to use and fill in that can make it easier to follow a particular family through the census, such as the free Ancestry downloads at **https://support.ancestry.co.uk/s/article/Free-Charts-and-Forms**.

How to find a 'lost' ancestor between the censuses
If you can't find an ancestor where you expect on the census, yet you have reason to believe they are still alive (for example, you've found them on a subsequent census or know their death was later) there are several things to try. Firstly, experiment with a few spelling variants in case the name has been mistranscribed, for example, substitute S for F, or try searching with a wildcard or part of the surname. If your website of choice allows it, try a Soundex search, which disregards vowels and some common consonants. It's also worth trying a phonetic spelling search, spelling the word the way it sounds when spoken. Often a harassed enumerator with many houses still to visit would have written down what he or she heard without bothering to check the exact spelling, particularly with unusual or foreign names.

Next, try searching for another person who you believe lives at the same address; this could lead you directly to the correct family and, hopefully, your missing person. If this doesn't work, try widening the net geographically. Could the person have moved area, perhaps for work, or even emigrated? Could they be staying with other family members elsewhere – perhaps helping with a newborn, or as a lodger. Is there a

If your ancestor goes 'missing' between censuses, consider that he or she might have been in prison. (© Wellcome Collection, public domain)

possibility they could be in a workhouse, prison or the military? Maybe in this decade they're working in service and living in a big house with other servants or were perhaps on holiday. Searching for the same name but with more of an open mind could set you on a new track.

Census Substitutes

Pre-national census records
The ten-year gap between censuses is, of course, a long period of time in the life of an ancestor; within a decade they could have moved house several times, got married, had children or passed away. Luckily, there are other records that act as census substitutes, some of which pre-date the first 1841 census, allowing you to explore the fortunes of pre-nineteenth-century ancestors.

For Yorkshire, a total of seventy-seven pre-1841 census records are known to exist for early censuses taken in 1801, 1811, 1821 and 1831 – the precursors of the full census. A free booklet by Richard Wall, Matthew Woollard and Beatrice Moring is available at **www.familyhistory.co.uk/pre-1841-census-records/** and this gives actual census schedules and listings for the Yorkshire parishes whose early returns survive, along with details of the information contained – ranging from a simple population number through to details of head of household, plus the number of occupants at the property; thankfully later censuses would go much further.

The 1939 Register
Despite the fact that the census is taken every ten years, as we saw earlier, an unfortunate set of events has impacted the availability of the mid-twentieth-century census for England when the next few come due for release under the 100-year closure rule. The wait until 2052 is a long one but, luckily, there are records to help close the gap.

Foremost among these is the 1939 Register, a valuable pre-war survey that includes full date of birth (rather than the year of birth asked on the census), address, occupation and marital status. When a woman married after the register had been taken, from the years 1948 to 1991, her married name was added to the register. A 100-year closure rule also applies to this register, unless it has been proven that the person in question has passed away. You can explore the register at Ancestry, Findmypast and TheGenealogist.

Electoral rolls/registers
Broadly speaking, electoral rolls or registers show the names of those entitled to vote – including, from 1928, an exact address. Although these records contain far less information than the census, because they were published annually, you can track an ancestor's whereabouts much more closely. The British Library holds the national collection of the registers; however, it describes the collection as 'patchy' before the First World War.

Electoral rolls, though, do continue through the twentieth century and you can also use trade town directories (explored more fully in Chapter 4) for those ancestors who ran a business. These publications were similar to a phone directory, in that they allowed readers to search for an individual, business or service. Many of these directories also carried advertisements, to allow a business to stand out from its competitors.

Findmypast's England and Wales, electoral registers collection is its single largest collection, with a total of 220 million voter names. Search by name, keyword, polling district, county or constituency at **https:// search.Findmypast.co.uk/search-world-records-in-census-land-and-surveys/and_electoral-rolls**.

Leeds Libraries website provides access to the Absent Voters List of 1918 **www.leeds.gov.uk/libraries/absent-war-voters** at which you can search by name for those whose home address was in the Leeds area. The full printed records are held at Leeds Central Library and can be copied/accessed by staff by paying a search fee.

Rate books and the hearth tax

Each parish collected rates, following Parliamentary Acts of 1597 and 1601, which formalised the rating system, to support the poor of the parish, and to pay for the upkeep of churches and roads. These rates were assessed based on the value of a dwelling, and details created of the occupier and owner of the house (which could be the same person), the amount of rent collected and the type of dwelling. From the eighteenth century onwards, these books act essentially as a directory of people on a particular street, and occasionally you may find comments about a particular house or property, in other cases it may simply be listed as a 'house'. Ancestry has a West Yorkshire rate books, accounts and censuses collection covering the years 1705 to 1893 at **www.ancestry.com/search/collections/9016/**.

Another means of obtaining the details of a head of household is via the hearth tax – particularly useful for seventeenth-century ancestors who lived before any English census was taken. The tax was introduced in 1662 and was based upon the number of hearths and ovens in a house. It was collected twice a year and because the occupier of the house, rather than the owner, was liable to pay, this can be a very useful record of ancestors who rented rather than owned property. Your ancestor might also be listed if he or she was exempt from paying the tax due to poverty.

Start your search at Hearth Tax Digital **https://gams.uni-graz.at/context:htx**, the home of the British Academy Hearth Tax Project at the

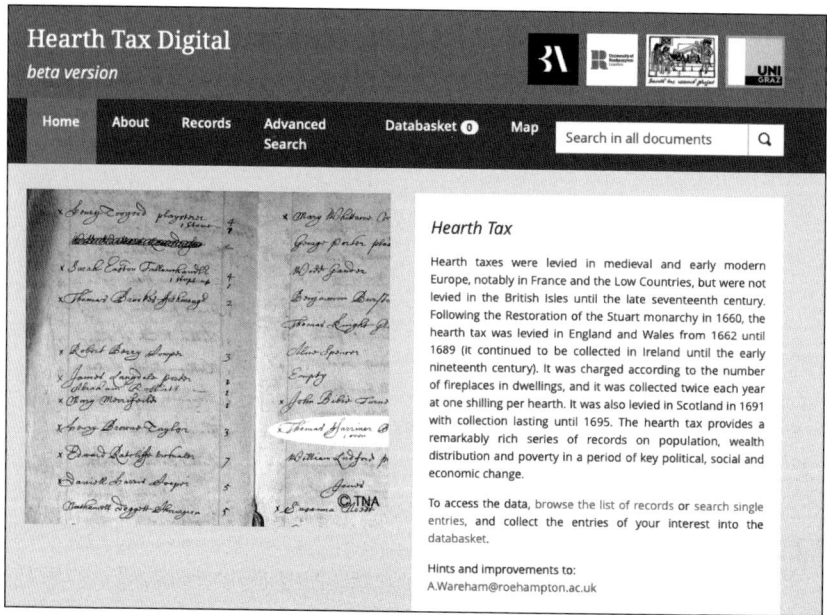

Hearth Tax Digital is a growing database of Yorkshire folk who paid this tax.

University of Roehampton. The records section of the site allows you to scan for the Yorkshire tax assessments, or you can search by name. You can place entries of interest into a data basket and then download into an Excel spreadsheet. This is an ongoing project and so is worth bookmarking, as new entries are added regularly. If you're able to track down a used copy of *Hearth Tax Returns for South Yorkshire, Ladyday, 1672* by David Hey and George Redmonds, this promises a wealth of Yorkshire surnames and information. The hearth tax was abolished in 1689 and replaced by the land tax, which we'll explore next.

Land Tax
The Land Tax followed on from the Hearth Tax and is another useful record for tracking the whereabouts of our pre-census ancestors. From 1692, this tax was administered across Britain on a local level and was eventually repealed in 1963. County record offices tend to hold these records and you can use the catalogue at FamilySearch under 'place search' to find your parish of interest, although many of these records are available only on microfilm at FamilySearch headquarters in the US, or at UK FamilySearch centres (find your nearest at **www.familysearch.org/centers/locations/**).

The Land Tax assessment was taken annually, meaning that you may be able to trace a proprietor across many years. Both property owner and tenant will usually be listed, with each person placed within a parish and a year. Most divisions are based upon the 1934–74 boundaries.

Ancestry, in conjunction with West Yorkshire Archive Service has Select Land Tax Records for 1704 to 1932 **www.ancestry.co.uk/search/collections/5108/** and these Land Tax books list all households in the areas and details such as who occupied the house, who owned the house, the name or situation of the property, and how much tax was collected. These records also include institutions such as schools and companies.

Deed registers
Deed registers document transactions that took place on a piece of land, showing who owned a particular piece of land or property. They tend to record transactions where land was held for twenty-five years or more, so can be a good way to keep track of less mobile ancestors. Although it wasn't compulsory to record land and property transactions such as these until 1897, many were documented and where they exist, they can be extremely enlightening.

Deeds for the West Riding cover the period 1704 to 1970 and are kept at the headquarters of WYAS, in Wakefield, running to several million deeds. East Riding deeds are kept at Beverley archives (1708–1976), whilst for those for the North Riding are at North Yorkshire County Record Office (1736–1970).

Whilst most of these records are accessible only at their respective record office, a limited number of North Riding Register of Deeds indexes have been transcribed as part of The Register of Deeds Project, an academic research project led by Dr Joan K.F. Heggie looking at women's involvement in property. This includes an index for Halifax for the period 1885–89 and the East Riding's Hull Index. Searchable transcriptions of North Riding Register of Deeds index registers for 1784–90 and 1885–89 are available online; as are all the 'M' townships for the period 1853–64, including Middlesbrough: **www.registerofdeeds.org.uk**.

Manorial documents

If you wish to trace back beyond the scope of parish records, then manorial documents provide a step further back into the past and, luckily, Yorkshire is well served. Manorial records, where they survive, provide the best chance of finding an ordinary person listed in estate archive material. Each medieval manor was part of an estate, an administrative unit that could be anything from a single parcel of land to huge tracts of countryside that included several parishes.

You might find your ancestor named in manorial records as a landowner, tenant, or perhaps someone who appeared in court or sat on a jury. The main caveat is these records are in Latin but if you are prepared to persevere, the rewards can be great. The National Archives has a guide to reading Latin at **www.nationalarchives.gov.uk/latin/** and several genealogy course providers also run courses periodically. You could also enlist the services of a professional researcher (see Chapter 9).

The University of Hull Archives at Hull History Centre holds a large collection of medieval manorial records and there is an excellent starter guide at **https://libguides.hull.ac.uk/common-record-types/manorial-records** which then links through to the online catalogue: **https://catalogue.hullhistorycentre.org.uk**.

Yorkshire is one of the few counties to have manorial records digitised and you can explore these on the Manorial Documents Register **https://discovery.nationalarchives.gov.uk/manor-search**. This is the official index to English and Welsh documents, giving their locations in both public and private hands. Manorial documents as defined in this register are described as 'court rolls, surveys, maps, terriers, documents and books of every description relating to the boundaries, franchises, wastes, customs or courts of a manor'. Title deeds are not included. You can search by historical county, standard manor name, alternative manor name, parish, or a combination of these.

Recently, the Healaugh and Muker manor court books, which cover a large area of Swaledale, have been made available in a project with the Swaledale and Arkengarthdale Archaeology Group. The court books are an invaluable source of information for local and family historians as they record all transfers of copyhold land within the manors, identifying the transferor, transferee and the property. They can be searched at **https://swaag.org/H&M-MCB-Intro.html** and currently cover the period 1686–1815, but will eventually be transcribed up to the 1920s.

House History

If your ancestors had a significant link to a property, or if you're interested in who might have lived in your house in years gone by, it's possible to make significant progress online. As with your own genealogy research, a house history can be as simple or as extensive as you wish. By using a combination of several resources explored above, including the census, electoral rolls and the hearth tax, together with some basic knowledge of building history, it's possible to tell the story of your chosen house over the decades and even centuries.

So how can you find out how old the house is? Sadly, here in the UK there is no central record of when individual properties were built, but there are places you can look to narrow down a date range. Old maps (covered in more depth in Chapter 10) can be a great help here as you can identify your property on the most up-to-date map you have and then work back through older maps until it no longer appears. Old Maps Online **www.oldmapsonline.org** is particularly useful.

Another site that may help is Ancestor Homes **www.ancestorhomes.com**, a collection of digitised documents relating to properties, going back as far as the seventeenth century. Search by surname, forename and with a date range or use the advanced search for street address and/or town. In a similar vein, Family Chest **www.familychest.co.uk** offers a free surname search of historical legal documents, including manorial court records, leases, sales and conveyances.

Old newspapers might also help, if all the houses on your street were built around a similar date. Older newspapers, and even more modern ones, often gave a place of residence in reports covering topics such as crime, celebrations like street parties, advertisements such as rental notices, awards and obituaries.

Could your house have appeared on an old postcard? Sites such as Tuck DB Postcards **https://tuckdbpostcards.org** have images of seemingly very 'ordinary' streets and so you may strike it lucky. The local history or heritage group may also have collections of old images. In a similar vein, community expertise can be tapped into with resources such as What Was There **www.whatwasthere.com**, which invites people to upload old photos relating to the history of their local area, with the images linked to Google Maps for easy searching.

Even quite 'ordinary' houses featured on the postcards of yesteryear. (© Tuck DB Postcards)

In terms of finding out about past inhabitants, the census and trade directories are your friends here, using them with a place rather than person search, and also use electoral registers to fill in the gaps. Ask around, too, either in person or on forums, as people who've lived on the street for a long time may have a wealth of information. You can follow a particular family through the censuses as they have children, those children grow up and move on, grandchildren perhaps come to stay and so on. Or if the moves are more frequent, it's interesting to see how often the property changes hands and the age and occupation of those who lived there.

Chapter 4

EDUCATION AND OCCUPATIONS

Work, whether paid or in the home, played a key role in the lives of many of our ancestors, just as it does today. The jobs that our forebears carried out will have determined their social status, income level and living standards. But before that came education, which we move to first.

Education

Before our ancestors embarked upon adult life, chances are that they experienced at least some years of schooling and then perhaps continued this childhood education via an apprenticeship, evening class or further education.

Most school records are deposited with county and local record offices and a small portion of these have been digitised. Such records can include admission registers and school log books, each of which may mention individual pupils and teachers, as well as details on the facilities of the school, the sort of education on offer – including the different subjects taught, and leisure provision such as school trips.

Your first step in tracing an ancestor's education is to work out which school or place of further education they might have attended, and then explore whether any records relating to that place have survived. If your ancestor lived in a village or small town, there may only be one or two possibilities; a city, with a wide range of educational establishments, could be more difficult. Commercial and trade directories often have lists of schools from the mid-nineteenth century onwards.

This FamilySearch guide **www.familysearch.org/en/wiki/England_ School_Records** provides a good starting point, with an explanation of England's schooling system over the centuries, as well as online resources, some of which we explore below.

If your interest is in a specific school, it's always worth Googling the school name with the word 'history' and also trying Facebook pages and local history groups for leads. You might also strike lucky and find a history of education for a specific region, such as 'The Yorkshire Dales in Victorian Times' on The Victorian Web **https://victorianweb.org/places/yorksdales/3.html**. Here, the author remarks upon the terrible reputation of Yorkshire schools in this era, thanks in part to the work of authors such as Charlotte Brontë (*Jane Eyre*) and Charles Dickens (*Nicholas Nickleby*) who portrayed spartan schools with downtrodden pupils and fearsome teachers.

Following a national project to digitise school admission registers and log books, Findmypast became the online home of records relating particularly to the years 1870 to 1914. The whole collection covers forty-one counties including Yorkshire, with 7 million records in total. Each record comprises a transcript and a colour image of the original register; the information held on each record varies but can include the pupil's name, year of birth, year of entry to the school, name and location of the school and the names of the parents. Explore at **https://search.Findmypast.co.uk/search-world-records/national-school-admission-registers-and-log-books-1870-1914**. I was lucky enough to find one of my ancestors in the collection and his details are below, to demonstrate what information can be gleaned:

> Tom Hanney, pupil at Halifax Parish Church from 4 August 1864. Record from the collection of Halifax WYAS. Notes: 'freehand prize in drawing exam'.

Of the two resources in this collection – school admission registers and log books – the latter, although it doesn't contain information on name or date of birth of pupils, makes for great reading, as local and even national occurrences can be mentioned, such as lesson plans, visitors to the school, outbreaks of illness and even the academic achievements of pupils. Admission registers, on the other hand, can be enlightening on the reason why a pupil left the school, ranging from moving away or experiencing health problems, through to the sad death of that child.

The school records of TheGenealogist go back centuries, with Yorkshire school registers as follows:

- 1499–1921   Giggleswick School
- 1546–1895   Sedbergh School
- 1820–1910   Leeds Grammar School
- 1875–1928   Sedbergh School
- 1914 and 1936   Bootham School

Several family history societies have also made good ground in digitising some of these registers, some of which can be found on the product pages of GenFair (**https://genfair.co.uk/**) to purchase as a book, booklet or download. Airedale & Wharfedale Family History Society (**https://awfhs.org**) is a great example of this type of project, and they have involved many of their members in a long-running project that began in 2009. Using the local knowledge of their members, they went beyond material held in county record offices by finding and recording admission registers from local studies libraries, museums, local history societies and those still held by the schools themselves. These registers were then filmed, either by the society or the local record office, and as a result of these endeavours, the registers of forty-three schools that are not found anywhere else online are now available to society members in a digitised format.

Newspapers can be a source of job adverts, news on exam successes, teachers attaining awards or retiring, and information on the running of school boards. Trade and street directories, too, can provide information on when a school opened, its size, teaching staff and its attendance figures.

British History Online has dozens of York schools listed in its 'schools and colleges' database **www.british-history.ac.uk/vch/yorks/city-of-york/pp440-460** taken from the 1951 text *A History of York*.

Occupations

In this section we take a look at an aspect of life that would have had a big impact on the quality of life, social status and even health of our ancestors: their occupation.

Of course, many of our ancestors missed out on the opportunities that we take for granted today – circumstances often meant that many had to take on whatever work was available, particularly in areas where there was one dominant industry, such as fishing, mining or textiles. So many of our forebears entered the mine or the mill because it was expected of them and there was little other work available.

Many also had to leave school at an early age in order to help the family survive; quite simply, families could not afford not to have everyone working as soon as each child reached the earliest school leaving age.

Over the next few pages, we'll take a look at how to find out an ancestor's occupation, explore the different records that can help you find out more, look at some of the most common Yorkshire occupations, and explore the various databases that have relevant documents and photographs.

How do I find out an ancestor's occupation?
If you're lucky, you might have inherited paperwork or memorabilia that can give you clues – perhaps a military medal or a certificate of long service. Older members of the family might also have memories or information that you then corroborate.

For nineteenth- and twentieth-century ancestors, the censuses and the 1939 Register give us a reliable guide across the decades. You could literally watch your ancestor move through the years from scholar, working as an apprentice and on to employment. Using this information in tandem with your ancestor's address you might even be able to use old maps to discern a potential workplace based on proximity to the home address.

Historical directories and trade directories are another good option for those ancestors who may have been self-employed. These publications had their heyday in the nineteenth century, and such was their popularity that they were often issued on an annual basis. The first of these directories was published in England in the seventeenth century, but most date from the eighteenth to twentieth centuries. The directories contain lists of tradespeople with their type of work and place of business, and sometimes an entry will be supplemented by an advertisement, giving further details about the type of business and its products. For example, you might find a shopkeeper ancestor listed across many years, moving into different premises and expanding the range of goods sold.

These publications also often included other information to attract subscribers – who paid to receive each edition of the directory – such as train timetables, details of market day in town, the times that postal collections were made, and an overview of the town and its facilities. The University of Leicester's database of local and trade directories for England and Wales runs from the 1760s to the 1910s and is arranged by county: **https://specialcollections.le.ac.uk/digital/collection/p16445coll4**. The Yorkshire page had, at the time of writing, fifty-three directories available to explore, covering the different Ridings of Yorkshire. Search by name, street, profession or other keyword. Even if you don't have an ancestor listed, these publications provide a great snapshot of a place in a given year, and are great to use alongside your census findings, or to explore a place before the start of the national census. The sheer range of trades is astonishing, for example the *Kelly's Directory of the North and East Ridings of Yorkshire* from 1893 has four pages of closely typed indexes to various occupations, starting with assurance and accountancy, on through iron gate handle manufacturers, garden seat manufacturers, margarine importers, silk mercers and finally zinc merchants. The Victorian era truly was the golden age of the British high street.

Local and trade directories can cover both urban and rural trades. (© Rare Book Division, The New York Public Library)

Both Ancestry and Findmypast have trade, commercial and residential directory collections at www.ancestry.co.uk/search/collections/3145/ and https://search.Findmypast.co.uk/search-world-Records/britain-business-indexes-1892-1987 respectively, with the latter including some photographs.

UKGDL **www.ukgdl.org.uk** is a great free site with more than 2,200 directories and lists. Start with 'select a county' on the left-hand menu and then enjoy browsing through a miscellany of genealogical materials, including ship passenger lists, lists of civil officials, poor rate records and many more.

Remember that birth, marriage and death records can also be a helpful source of occupation information, as can wills. As well as providing a maiden surname for the mother (in itself a valuable research stepping stone) birth certificates also include the father's occupation. On marriage certificates, you should be able to find occupations (where applicable) for bride, groom and both fathers. Death certificates also sometimes include the occupation of the deceased.

Local newspapers, too, are a rich source of information and if you're lucky, maybe even photographs. Possible events that could have been recorded include a long service award, business advertisement, prize or competition win at work, a promotion and even, sadly, perhaps a bankruptcy. Remember that local and national newspapers were a key source of information for our nineteenth- and twentieth-century ancestors and even what may seem fairly trivial events, such as a works Christmas party or trip to the seaside, might have been written about and photographed.

The Gazette website has thousands of insolvency notices dating back to the 1700s, and these are free to access, with a guide to their use at **www.thegazette.co.uk/all-notices/content/100812**. As noted in the guide, the financial misfortune of your ancestor can be to your advantage, as you could find details including place of residence, previous addresses, occupation, notice of goods stocked within the business and so on.

If you're planning to use the main commercial websites to carry out some of your research, Ancestry has a video on searching its occupation records **www.ancestry.co.uk/cs/start-occupations**, whilst the Findmypast gateway page can be found at **https://search.Findmypast.co.uk/search-united-kingdom-records-in-education-and-work**.

What was their job?

Before we delve into the resources available for a number of Yorkshire trades and industries, let's look at how to find out more about an unfamiliar job title that you may encounter on the census, a marriage certificate or in a newspaper, for example.

Genuki has a good UK database that references various non-digital, old and/or out-of-print books that you can try to source. These are ideal if you know the name of an ancestor's occupation but are less familiar with what that work would have involved: **www.genuki.org.uk/big/Occupations**. This section of the site also directs you to further source materials, some of which you may be able to find online, e.g. at Google Books, second-hand retailers etc.

Both FamilySearch **www.familysearch.org/en/wiki/England_Occupations** and Dictionary of Old Occupations on the Family Researcher website **www.familyresearcher.co.uk/glossary/Dictionary-of-Old-Occupations-Index.html** have alphabetical occupation lists, with the latter comprising some 2,000 occupations, surely one of the most comprehensive on the web. From All Spice (seller of foodstuffs) to Zythepsarist (who brewed alcohol) it's informative and fun to explore.

With regard to occupations unique to, or prevalent in, Yorkshire, Bradford Historical Society has an interesting article by Elvira Willmott originally published in 1989 **www.bradfordhistorical.org.uk/occupations.html** on jobs in eighteenth-century Bradford. The earliest information comes from baptism registers, which show fathers' occupations from 1713 through to 1775. Textiles predominate, as you might expect, but coal mining, brewing, nail-making and ropemaking are also featured. The methods by which the author obtained this information are also explained, which is very helpful in terms of learning how to carry out similar research for other towns.

The Society of Genealogists (SoG) has many occupation-related records available to its members, for example, collections relating to occupations such as coastguards, mariners in the Trinity House petitions, and teachers. Members can search across most of the society's digital collections by name at the SoG website: **www.sog.org.uk/our-collections/**. If you aren't a member, you can search for free and then take out a membership if you find something promising that you wish to access. Keep a look out, too, for the society's 'My ancestor was a —' series of books, available from its online shop and other book retailers. These comprehensive guides have lots of information on various industries, the related records and different search strategies.

If your ancestor was an industrial worker, the Pistol, Pen & Press database **www.pistonpenandpress.org/database/** allows you to search and browse records of industrial workers and literary culture across the north of England. The resource has entries for individuals, for literary works (many including transcriptions of poems, songs or prose extracts) and for associations that sponsored literary activities and were connected to industry.

Women and work
Women, of course, can be found in most of the occupations we're about to explore; however, before we look at these records it's worth being aware of their possible limitations when it comes to tracing female ancestors. As with so much of history, records were written by men and

Fordson tractor with members of the British Land Army. (© Fox Photos, public domain)

about men. So, whilst of course you'll find your female ancestors on BMD certificates, the census and so on, woman have traditionally until the last half century or so, worked in lower paid, temporary or menial roles. Workers in jobs such as domestic service, corner shops and textile mills may not have left their mark on an employment record.

In many ways, this is also true of our male ancestors. It's easy to assume that 'somewhere out there' will be lists of employees, records of service, pension documents and so on. However, the search for employment details is more about building up a picture of the job role, working conditions and benefits, and possible employers, rather than actually finding an ancestor named in those records; if you do so it will be a bonus. Your best hope for finding a named ancestor is for those who worked as a sole proprietor or employed others. The search is still worthwhile, however, and can yield plenty of information, so let's move on to some of the major Yorkshire industries.

Mining

Although mining took place across all three Ridings, it is perhaps most associated with South Yorkshire. Even areas that we would now consider to be rural and picturesque might have once been home to mines and their communities, as this Yorkshire Dales coalfields map from Northern Mine Research Society shows: **www.nmrs.org.uk/mines-map/coal-mining-in-the-british-isles/yorkshire-coalfield/yorkshiredales/**.

A key resource for mining is the website of the National Coal Mining Museum near Wakefield which, as well as its fascinating museum and underground tours, is home to a nationally recognised library and special collections. The main online provision is the digitised copies of *Coal Magazine*, accessed from the catalogue page **www.ncm.org.uk/library/**. These run from 1947 to the mid-1960s and are searchable by keyword and year, or you can browse issue by issue. Viewing the different front covers of the magazine over the years is like stepping back in time, with images of families, miners, industrial machinery, coal mines, musicians and beauty queens; all looking back on an era of community cohesion, pride in the industry, and of course, times of struggle and strife. Inside are adverts aimed at this specialised readership, local news and gossip, items of national concern and spotlights on individual pits.

The library catalogue provides details of 20,000 items; however, these are only available from the library at the museum site in Wakefield, and so of limited use for online research.

The Northern Mine Research Society **www.nmrs.org.uk** is dedicated to the preservation and recording of mining history and despite its name, its focus is countrywide. On the website you can find a Yorkshire Dales coalfields map; a page of Yorkshire records, with notes on where these can be found; a page of articles and resources relating to all forms of mining in England; and a searchable mining accidents map.

If your mining ancestors came from the Kirklees area of West Yorkshire, Kirklees Cousins **https://kirkleescousins.co.uk/crime-and-punishment/** is of interest for both coal and textile kin. Here, you will find a good overview of coal mining in Yorkshire and an account of the Combs Colliery Disaster of 4 July 1893. This poignant tale demonstrates how far-reaching the impacts of such a disaster could be in a close-knit community that relied on mining for its livelihood. In all, a total of 139 miners ranging in age from 12 to 70 years were killed in the disaster. A fund set up in the aftermath attracted donations from across the country and more than £30,000 was raised, which was shared out between the widows and orphans affected. Despite the payouts, life would have been financially hard for those who lost a loved one, as the report explains:

Unless they could re-marry, the widows would suffer great hardship. As coal hewers, most of their menfolk would be earning a good wage compared to labourers above ground ... given six shifts worked each week, that would be a wage of £1 16s each week, almost five times the payout that the widows would receive.

Maritime industries

With its 45-mile coastline, encompassing globally known fishing towns and ports such as Hull and Scarborough, many of our forebears would have earned their living from the ocean, or perhaps just supplemented their diet or earnings from the bounty of the North Sea. Until the coming of the railways, fish was a foodstuff reserved only for the wealthy, or for those who lived close to the coast. However, as the eighteenth century progressed and urban populations grew, large numbers of people needed to be fed at low cost and fish began to used widely as a cheap and plentiful food source, with fishermen finding their services in great demand.

Records for the town of Hull are a case in point. In 1840, there were just seven fishing vessels registered, ten years later there were thirty-five, with this number climbing to 177 in 1860 and 400 by 1878.

Yorkshire fisher folk. (© Rare Book Division, The New York Public Library)

Hull City Archives has a large maritime collection and its fishing and maritime hub page **https://hullhistorycentre.org.uk/research/research-guides/browse-fishing-and-maritime.aspx** offers access to related research guides, histories of whaling and the Hull docks, and fishing crew lists, skipper cards and muster rolls – the latter two a name-rich resource – although you would need to visit the archives or use its paid research service to access the information should you find an ancestor named in the indexes.

'Scarborough fishing families' **www.scarboroughsmaritimeheritage.org.uk/article.php?article=385** on the Scarborough Maritime Heritage Centre has a number of evocative reads, including an A to Z of famous Scarborough people, and an account of the Filey, Flamborough and Runswick Bay coble fishing boats which, after a catch, were pulled out from the sea as a community effort, with men, women and older children helping in the days before tractors were used. These cobles were well adapted to work on the Yorkshire coast, picking up crabs and lobsters in spring and running around the choppy seas in the summer and autumn. They were even fleet enough to enter the caves of Flamborough Head with paying passengers during the summer holiday season.

For more nostalgia the Yorkshire Film Archive **www.yfanefa.com** offers a great insight into this way of life, with films and documentaries covering the boats and workers of the maritime industry.

The 'Trawling Through Time' project blog **https://trawlingthroughtime.org/** from East Riding Archives relates to the history of Cook, Welton & Gemmell, shipbuilders of Beverley (1901–63). Once the largest trawler manufacturer in the world, it employed hundreds of people in the town.

In a similar vein, Hornsea Pottery **www.eastridingarchives.co.uk/archives-online/hornsea-pottery** is an exhibition on the history of

Two ATS (Auxiliary Territorial Service) trainee motorcycle despatch riders and a Royal Army Service Corps instructor at York, 23 May 1941. (Photograph by E.G. Malindine (War Office official photographer), public domain)

an internationally renowned pottery works and visitor attraction that operated in the town of Hornsea in the mid-to late twentieth century.

Military

Whether working in the armed forces as a career, or enlisting during wartime or as a volunteer, many British families will have at least one ancestor who served in the military. However, this type of research can seem daunting if you're not used to the terminology. This is where online research is so useful, as you can familiarise yourself with some of the key terms and facts before you delve deeper and look for records that may feature your forebears.

Each of the main subscription-based websites has a selection of military records. TheGenealogist has 15th Foot Regiment (East Riding) historical records, records for officers of the Green Howards covering 1688 to 1931, and also 19th Foot Regiment (North Riding). At Ancestry, the UK military records collections can be found at **www.ancestry.co.uk/search/categories/uk_military_collections/** and a number of these are marked as free to use, including First World War medal rolls index cards, D-Day diaries and photographs, and the Royal Navy Division Index for 1914–19. Findmypast has over 60 million military and conflict records, including civil war and rebellion, regimental and service records, and war-related directories and almanacs. Military nurses, volunteer soldiers and army deserters are also included.

Another good resource is Forces War Records **www.forces-war-records.co.uk**, which has 27 million records as well as World War timelines, campaign medal guides and regiment histories. Since May 2021, the site has been part of the Ancestry group. If you find a record of interest, the site also includes linked information, for example with details of the ship the person served on, a battle they were involved in, or a medal they were awarded. The basic membership is free and you can also take out a monthly or annual subscription for full, unrestricted access and exclusive records and documents.

MyHeritage has forty-one UK military collections **www.myheritage.com/records/United-Kingdom/military-records** covering the period 1700 to the 2000s, including lists of war badge recipients, PoW records, Boer War casualty lists and Victoria Cross recipients 1854 to 2006.

If you'd like to use these subscription sites and are not a member, keep your eyes open at key dates such as Remembrance Day, as many of the records are offered as free to use for a specific short period.

Moving on to non-subscription sites, Steve Whitwam's extensive family history site **www.whitwam.co.uk/war.htm** for the Colne Valley in Huddersfield is packed full of useful information, including a First World War project that features a list of Colne Valley soldiers taken from a 1918 almanac. Many of the entries include a photograph and you can also find detailed information including names of parents, birth town, military service, address and even peacetime hobbies. For example:

> Lieut. ARNOLD McLINTOCK, Duke of Wellington's W. R. Regt., was reported as missing on the 3rd of Sept., 1916, but in the February following information was received from the War Office that he had been killed on the date previously given. He was the son of the late Dr. McLintock, formerly in practice at Marsden, and a nephew of Mr. Harold Fisher, of Lingards Wood House, Marsden, with whom he resided. Before the outbreak of war he was a partner in the Ramsden Mill Co., Linthwaite.

The Wakefield We Will Remember Them website has a searchable name index **www.wakefield.gov.uk/libraries-and-local-history/local-and-family-history/we-will-remember-them/name-index** with quite extensive wartime service details for many of the men featured, including some photographs. Some of these also go on to relate post-war life, including marriage and the birth of children.

Imperial War Museum **www.iwm.org.uk/memorials/search** is also a good site, particularly the IWM War Memorials register with 8,000 Yorkshire entries, many of which are in places you might not think to look, such as the Lancashire and Yorkshire Railway Carriage and Wagons department memorial at the Oldham Road Carriage and Wagon Works in Newton Heath, and Women of the Three Yorkshire Ridings memorial in Hull Railway Station. Each entry has a photo where available, background history, current location, OS grid reference, a description, inscription, number of names on the memorial, specific conflict if applicable and more.

For the Yorkshire Women's Land Army, visit the Borthwick Institute for Archives project page **www.york.ac.uk/borthwick/projects/fertilegroundrecordsofthewomenslandarmyinnorthyorkshire/** for details of the project, which began in 2021, to catalogue and make publicly available the records of Lady Celia Milnes Coates and her work with the Women's Land Army in North Yorkshire. You can find descriptions of the records on the Borthcat catalogue, listen to a podcast about the archive and arrange to access the collection at The Borthwick.

UK Military Family History **www.ukmfh.org.uk** and its sister site UK Genealogical Directories and Lists **www.ukgdl.org.uk** provide links to thousands of websites that can help you with military family history. UK MFH has more than 1,500 links to records that include muster rolls, discharge papers and pension records. The latter website also has its own occupations and apprenticeships site, with an advanced search facility and a truly impressive range of occupations to search – from abbot, through dredgerman and magnesia manufacturer and on to zoologist.

One of the categories on UK Military Family History is museums – don't discount this if you aren't able to visit the museums that come up in your search as many will have online resources, or be able to connect you with a specialised researcher who can undertake paid research on your behalf. Indeed, military history is one of the areas where having the help of a professional can be really worthwhile because of the specialist records and terms, and the fact that most of us don't use military records with the same regularity as those for 'everyday' ancestors.

Rotherham Archives is the archive repository for the York and Lancaster Regiment and recently had records from 1899 to 1930 digitised and launched online via The Ogilby Muster at **www.theogilbymuster.com/york_lancaster_regiment_museum**. You need to register (free) to use the site, the only charge is if you wish to purchase a copy of an image. The archive itself, which is based at Clifton Park Museum in Rotherham, covers the history of the regiment and of its forebears – the 65th and 84th regiments of foot. There are more than 18,400 items to explore online.

First World War Lives from East Riding Archives **www.eastridingarchives.co.uk/ww1lives/** is an ongoing project that has now featured more than 1,000 servicemen, whose lives have been researched and details added to the online database. The lives are arranged under a range of headings, including women in war, teenagers in service, as well as British Army, Royal Navy and Royal Air Force. You can browse the online catalogue from the home page, or download the personnel list as an Excel document or PDF.

Ancestry has a number of military records from West Yorkshire Archive Service, **www.ancestry.co.uk/search/collections/8545/** including West Yorkshire militia 1779–1826, which includes a variety of militia-related records, including township payments to the militia, lists of officers, and lists of eligible men. Individual records can include a militiaman's name, a date and location, occupation, age range, number of children, any infirmities, and signature. Some of these records also include exemptions for 'effective volunteers' (those already serving in another capacity as a volunteer), poor men with children, clergy, teachers, apprentices, constables, peace officers, those who hired substitutes, and those who were infirm, among others.

In terms of those who did not fight, the North Yorkshire Record Office catalogue includes thousands of names of individuals, including details of the case papers of 6,000 men who appeared before the North Riding Tribunal to appeal against conscription in the First World War: **archivesunlocked.northyorks.gov.uk**.

The Second World War Experience Centre in Otley, West Yorkshire, is an archive that collects and preserves the surviving testimonies of those who lived during the Second World War. This includes an international collection of *c.*5,000 recorded interviews and over 6,000 entries of donated material from service personnel and civilians, including women and children. The holdings of the archive are available to historians, researchers, authors, and all those interested in the Second World War. Visit **www.war-experience.org** to see an overview of the archive's collections and for contact details. A searchable online digital catalogue is currently in being created for the website. Research queries are welcome and can be made at **https://war-experience.org/help-with-research/**, via the archive's social media platforms which include Facebook, Instagram @secondworldwararchive, and Twitter @SWWEC1.

Staying in West Yorkshire, University of Leeds Library has a fine collection of First World War propaganda posters **at https://library.leeds.ac.uk/special-collections/tour/726/war_propaganda#activate-image1**. These are part of the Liddle Collection, which documents and preserves the first-hand accounts of those who experienced the two world wars – both men and women, those who were and weren't members of the armed forces, and also non-British individuals. You can search the indexes at **https://explore.library.leeds.ac.uk/special-collections-explore/Liddle%20Collection%20Index** and then access individual items at the university.

Textiles

The textile trade was a huge employer; however, there are comparatively few records relating to individual employees, unless your ancestor was someone important within the trade. Nevertheless, there are some really colourful and evocative records to explore, and plenty of visual inspiration too.

As mentioned in the coal mining section, Kirklees Cousins **https://kirkleescousins.co.uk/cloth-market-and-cloth-halls/** is also useful for its essays on the rise and expansion of the West Yorkshire wool trade, its exploration of the shoddy and mungo industries, which were waste wool industries whereby waste woollen products were shredded into fibres that were then mixed with wool to blend into new fibres to be woven into cloth. Brighouse and Ossett were noted centres for this work.

There is also an interesting feature on the West Yorkshire cloth halls, many of which still stand today, and which would have been a familiar haunt for any of our forebears who bought or sold cloth.

One of Yorkshire's most famous textile communities was Saltaire, the model village created by Sir Titus Salt and now a World Heritage Site. The village was created to house mill workers from the nearby town of Bradford and its two mills and accompanying housing, leisure facilities and church provided a self-contained community and offered an escape from the slum conditions many Bradford textile workers were forced to endure. Saltaire Collection **www.saltairecollection.org** is the online home of the archive and offers a good overview of the archive collection and its accompanying learning resources.

There are more than 6,000 items in the collection including documents, photos, maps, newspaper cuttings books and objects, spanning a period from the 1850s through to the present day. The catalogue **www.saltairecollection.org/explore-the-collection/whole-collection/** is in the process of being updated and more items digitised. At the time of writing, the vast majority of the collection was not available to view digitally; however, the 'Saltaire's History' section of the website provides a great introduction to Sir Titus Salt, the mills, village, leisure facilities and the heritage of continuing education.

And as with the industries above, be sure to visit Yorkshire Film Archive for evocative footage including royal mill visits, mill trips to the seaside and documentaries on textiles and textile production. *Albert's Last Skip* is a twenty-eight-minute film from 1978 that chronicles the process of making skeps – wicker baskets that were used to deliver yarn to Yorkshire's mills. Seventy-three-year-old Albert Gaff of Eccleshall talks about his working life, details how skeps were made, and talks about the tools he used.

Railways

A good way to start in this subject area is the National Archives research guide **www.nationalarchives.gov.uk/help-with-your-research/research-guides/railway-workers/** covering workers such as engine drivers, office and warehouse workers and typists. As you might expect, fewer records were created – or have survived – for casual workers, those who worked on the construction of the railways, and the 'navvies'. Also, personnel records for staff who worked for the railways in the post-war period from 1948 have not survived. County record offices may have some staff record cards with summaries of employment.

Ancestry's records cover some of the main railway companies including Great Western, Great Central, and London, Midland and Scottish Railways.

The City of York is home to the National Railway Museum – the national collection of rail history **www.railwaymuseum.org.uk**. It has a library called The Search Engine **www.railwaymuseum.org.uk/ research-and-archive**, which you can visit at the museum (check website for opening times and how to access resources) and some of which can be accessed online. The Search Engine also offers a paid-for research service for those unable to visit, or who would like help navigating the various records available. The further resources guides include links to relevant books, and there is also a family history section of the site **www.railwaymuseum.org.uk/research-and-archivefurther-resources/ family-history**, which has many links to further online resources. The excellent resource packs are full of advice, including one which links to the Science and Society picture library for railway-related images **www.ssplprints.com**.

The museum is also involved with two major projects: The Railway Work, Life and Death project where staff are building up a database of railway worker accidents **www.railwayaccidents.port.ac.uk/** alongside researchers at the University of Portsmouth and the Modern Records Centre at the University of Warwick; and the Fallen Railwaymen site, which provides information on more than 20,000 railway workers who died in military service during the First World War: **https:// fallenrailwaymen.omeka.net/**.

And finally, there are currently two Future Learn free distance learning courses: Working Lives on the Railway **www.futurelearn. com/courses/working-lives-on-the-railway** and the Rise of the Railway Station **www.futurelearn.com/courses/railway-history-the-rise-of-the-railway-station**. Created in association with the University of Strathclyde, they provide useful historical context for family historians and run periodically.

Chapter 5

TOUGH TIMES: ILL HEALTH, POVERTY AND CRIME

Although we hope that our ancestors had long and happy lives, the tough times they went through in life can often prove very fruitful in terms of a genealogy paper trail.

Poverty and Ill Health

Forebears who fell upon hard times or experienced illness may well have left their mark on the records, and distressing though these stories can be, such ancestors can be easier to trace than those who made their way between birth and death with few unpleasant incidents.

As Stuart Raymond explains in *Tracing Your Poor Ancestors* (Pen & Sword, 2020), the main records where we will find out poor ancestors are those that relate to the poor law, charity (i.e. when individual paupers received financial aid) and crime. For a long time, poverty was in effect treated as a crime, with people punished for nothing more than vagrancy and begging, not to mention those whose circumstances pushed them towards crime – from stealing a loaf of bread to feed starving family members, to falling into a life of crime in order to survive after a period of unemployment or illness.

Since the mid-sixteenth century, England has had a poor law system that aimed not only to aid those who fell upon hard times but also protect the population at large from being overwhelmed by the needs of the poor. Until 1834, individual areas of Yorkshire had responsibility for law and order within their own particular boundaries. This included the administration of charitable benefits, and caring for the poor, sick and aged. Yorkshire differs from the rest of England in that the unit of administration was a township rather than a parish. Poverty and poor relief are examined in a useful guide at Connected Histories **www.connectedhistories.org/guide/7/** where you can read about the background to the various poor laws, their strengths and weaknesses, as well as anecdotes and life histories.

The main record types for tracing ancestors in poverty are settlement certificates, examinations, letters from the poor asking for assistance, parish minute books, quarter session records, pauper apprenticeship records and workhouse records – all of which will potentially include the name and other details of individuals. The National Archives' 'Poverty and the Poor Law' guide **www.nationalarchives.gov.uk/help-with-your-research/research-guides/poverty-poor-laws/#3-how-to-find-records-before-1834** helps with both pre- and post-poor law research. As the birth of Poor Law Unions in 1834 created the workhouse system, with its own form of records; most pre-poor law records are held by local archives and county records. By no means all have been digitised and most will be subject to a 100-year closure period.

Casual work was the lot of many, often travelling from place to place to find employment on roads or railways. © Rare Book Division, The New York Public Library. 'Stone breakers on the road'. (The New York Public Library Digital Collections, 1814–1813)

Both Ancestry and Findmypast have some settlement certificates and removal records, with Ancestry covering West Yorkshire 1689 to 1866, and Findmypast with Sheffield settlement certificates for 1558 to 1939. Removal and settlement records, where they survive, can provide valuable family information, often extending to more than one generation. The right to settlement allowed the person concerned to claim poor relief in that place because townships and parishes were unwilling to pay for anyone not born within their borders or with a right to settlement, for example through marriage or renting property. The questions asked of the person claiming settlement were probing and thus provide us with information such as places and dates of former and current residence, details of spouse and children, and grounds for settlement or removal.

West Yorkshire is again well served on Ancestry with its 'select poor law and township records 1663–1914' collection that includes churchwardens' records, relief records, payments to mothers of illegitimate children, lunatic registers and workhouse records: **www.ancestry.co.uk/search/collections/9017/**.

Yorkshire's Poor Law Unions are listed at FamilySearch **www.familysearch.org/en/wiki/Yorkshire_Poor_Law_Unions** and this page also refers the reader to Peter Higginbotham's hugely helpful and unequalled Workhouses website. The site's Poor Law Unions Yorkshire map **www.workhouses.org.uk/map/yorks.shtml** is a good starting point, and from here you can find your parish/area and then click on that place of interest to go through to a page of information, stories and photographs relating to the workhouse(s) within that location. Most of these entries have information on where to find details of staff, inmates, workhouse records, further reading and online links. The original records are from the various offices of West Yorkshire Archive Service.

For example, the Pocklington Workhouse page **www.workhouses.org.uk/Pocklington/** refers to the 1881 census for staff details and inmates; there is another internal page of inmates and ages in 1861; records at East Riding of Yorkshire Archives, and a link to the Ripon Workhouse Museum (**https://riponmuseums.co.uk/workhouse-museum-garden/**) which has stories of inmates, details of a workhouse diet, and a history of this workhouse. This website is a treasure trove of background information on workhouse life, with details of rules, work, clothing, punishment, medical care, death and how inmates were 'classified' within the system. The site is free to use and donations are welcome.

Local newspapers can also be a fruitful source of workhouse information, with reports on topics such as Christmas Day fare for inmates, through to scandals and court cases relating to staff and inmates. The *British Banner* of 18 July 1849 ran a short news story on the 'remarkable longevity' of the inmates of Hull Workhouse, reporting that the combined age of the 290 inmates receiving relief was 20,958 years, giving an average age of 72, with the women ranging in age from 60 to 96, and the men 61 through to 93.

The tale of a monotonous diet was related in the 14 January 1914 *Sheffield Independent*, whilst the story of former 'lord of the manor' Joshua Illingworth dying at Pudsey Workhouse was reported in *The Scotsman* of 8 June 1912.

The 1834 Poor Law Act also made provision for assisted emigration, and this may prove a fruitful line of enquiry if you lose sight of an ancestor in the English records. Not everyone was sent overseas, however. Of particular note for those whose ancestors arrived in Yorkshire during the 1830s was the Migration Agency of this decade, which was tasked with sending rural paupers from the south of England in need of poor relief to northern industrial towns such as Leeds and Bradford, where they might readily find employment, particularly in the textile trade. My own Scarfe ancestors arrived in Yorkshire from Suffolk in such circumstances, something I only became aware of after finding their Suffolk birthplaces on the 1861 Bradford census and unravelling the circumstances that had led them to this Victorian town at the height of the Industrial Revolution. Situations such as this one may be found in the parish minute books – check with your county record office about survival and availability.

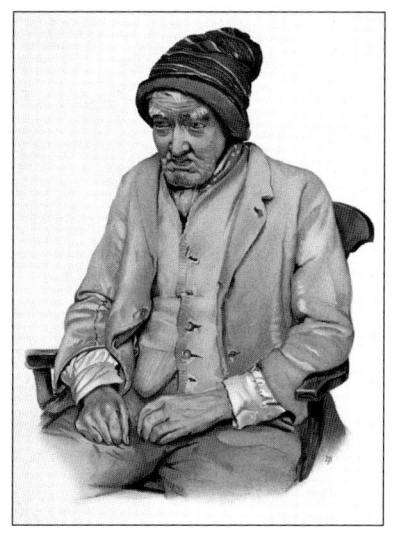

The elderly were often forced to end their days in the workhouse if no family member could offer support. (© Wellcome Collection, public domain mark)

The Retreat Archive at Wellcome Collection **https://wellcomecollection. org/works/ev6qtxjs** comprises material relating to the Retreat Hospital, a Quaker-run private asylum founded in York in 1792. Large parts of the collection, including administrative and patient records, were digitised for the Wellcome Collections. The collection itself is unusually complete, with extensive records for both staff and patients. The former include applications for posts, lists of duties and time books, whilst patients are represented through letters, diaries and detailed case notes.

Crime
Your first indication that an ancestor was convicted of a crime might be if you search for the person on the census and find him or her listed as

a prisoner at one of the county's jails. Or perhaps you've followed up on a half-forgotten family story and discovered an ancestor's criminal past via newspaper reports. Either way, there are several ways in which you can find out more about an ancestor who was a victim, witness or perpetrator of a crime.

To start your search, you'll need to work out which record office holds the records for your police force of interest, and then find out what records are available online. Generally, this will mean visiting the website for the record office and/or local history library for your place of interest, searching the catalogue and either exploring the material online, or enquiring about a research service. In addition, below are some specialised guides for various areas of the county.

For South Yorkshire, Sheffield has a PDF research guide **https://bit.ly/3DqI9LH** that explains the history of policing in Sheffield, where information on police officers and criminals can be found, and the location of court records. Picture Sheffield **www.picturesheffield.com** has related images.

For North Yorkshire, Google Books has copies of volumes of quarter session records produced by the North Riding Record Society. These run into hundreds of pages and are searchable. Volume 1 can be found at **https://bit.ly/4732298**. You can use this link to explore the subsequent volumes. Also visit archive.org for a digitised copy of Court of Quarter Sessions of the Peace (Yorkshire, North Riding) published in 1884: **https://archive.org/details/quartersessionr02atkigoog**.

North Yorkshire County Record Office also has a fascinating blog **https://nycroblog.com/category/collections/quarter-sessions/** on the life and times of a selection of 'criminal women', including the tale of a 5-week old baby sent in a parcel by train from Middlesbrough to Guisborough, from a quarter session case heard on 25 August 1869. The infant was sent inside a hamper by Martha and Mary Falkingham, according to the court session report, to a George Beaumont, whom the women accused of having fathered the baby by Mary. The mother and daughter accused George of refusing to take responsibility for the child – an accusation he denied, saying that he had offered to marry Mary. Mary and her mother were sentenced to a month's hard labour for 'unlawfully and wilfully abandoning and exposing a child whereby the life of the said child was endangered' and sadly, the child died at Guisborough Workhouse a few weeks after the court case, although apparently not from the effects of its journey.

Ancestry's Register of Habitual Criminals and Police Gazettes 1834–1934 comprises registers and weekly newspapers with details of criminals, including habitual criminal registers, photographs and physical descriptions for the Victorian era and beyond: **https://bit.ly/3Q55wSL**. It also has West Yorkshire police records for 1833 to 1914, which includes registers of the appointment of regular and special constables, transfers, some physical descriptions and in some records, details of birth date and place, plus name of spouse.

Also at Ancestry are the Prisons and Calendars of Prisoners records 1801–1914 **www.ancestry.co.uk/search/collections/5085/** which covers Wakefield prison, and its prisoners, who came from across the West Riding. Originally known as the West Riding House of Correction and built in 1595, its buildings were replaced in the 1760s and in 1847. Twenty-seven years later, it became part of the national prisons system as HM Prison Wakefield. Your search will show prisoner's name, sentence, nature of offence and previous offences. You may also be lucky enough to find other information on family members, residence, physical appearance and education.

If your West Yorkshire ancestor fell into crime at a young age they may have gone to one of the area's reformatory schools: Calder Farm Reformatory, East Moor Community Home School or Shadwell Children's Centre. The years covered in this collection are 1856, through to 1914, which is the privacy cut-off point: **www.ancestry.co.uk/search/collections/8633/**.

Each of the above records was supplied with the assistance of West Yorkshire Archive Service.

At Findmypast you can find England and Wales, Crime, Prisons and Punishment 1770–1935 **https://search.Findmypast.co.uk/search-world-records/england-and-wales-crime-prisons-and-punishment-1770-1935** a collection of 5 million records on criminals who passed through the justice system, including the sentence given and what life was like in prison. If you're fortunate, you might come across a photograph of your ancestor and a sample of their handwriting. When carrying out your search, select 'place' as one of the search parameters and a drop-down menu will show the assize records for locations including Leeds, Beverley, Bradford and the North Riding.

Court proceedings
Ancestry has Yorkshire quarter session records for the period 1637 to 1914 – covering criminal cases heard in Bradford, Halifax, Huddersfield and Wakefield. Many of the cases run across several pages, so be sure to use the arrow function to browse the surrounding pages. Findmypast has quarter sessions for Sheffield for 1880–1912, comprising more than 11,000 records.

Prisoner at court. (© Wellcome Collection, public domain)

For North Yorkshire, the York Cause Papers Database searchable catalogue of more than 14,000 cause papers **www.dhi.ac.uk/causepapers/** relating to cases heard between 1300 and 1858 in the Church Courts of the diocese of York. The original records are held in the Borthwick Institute for Archives at the University of York, and are the most extensive records of their type in the UK.

Not all records relating to crime relate to the county; some more serious crimes were tried elsewhere. Old Bailey Online **www.oldbaileyonline.org** is a fully searchable edition of the proceedings of London's central criminal court between 1674 and 1913. This collection of more than 197,000 records of non-elite people is a sobering reminder of centuries gone by, when even a seemingly trivial misdemeanour could be severely punished:

> 9 April 1684
> Katharine Smith, known amongst the Pick-Pocket by the name of Yorkshire Kate, was Indicted for stealing Handkerchiefs and other linnen, of the Goods of Thomas Williams, and found Guilty of Felony and Burglary.

Katharine was sentenced to death.

> **Top tip**
> Use the Internet Archive (and Google Books) to download digitised books, which for Yorkshire includes all the Yorkshire Archaeological Society Record Series up to volume 130+, together with the first fifteen volumes of the Wakefield Court Roll Series.
>
> Steven Bruce, Yorkshire Family History
(www.yorkshirefamilyhistory.org)
>
> For more on the court rolls and their importance see **www.yas.org.uk/Publications/Wakefield-Court-Rolls-Series**.

If your search of Old Bailey Online leads you to an ancestor who was deported, you can continue your research at Digital Panopticon **www.digitalpanopticon.org** to discover what happened to the person next.

Newspapers

As in so many areas of family history research, historical newspapers are a rich source of names and places, and of course because crime sells, these periodicals were keen to fill their pages with accounts of arrests, trials and convictions. As well as British Newspaper Archive both *The Times* (1785–1985) **www.thetimes.co.uk/archive** and *The Guardian* **http://guardian.calmview.eu/CalmView/default.aspx** have digital archives. Within these pages you have access to tens of thousands of cases, from petty theft through to murder. Many of the trial proceedings explain the process in detail, allowing you to build up a picture of the legal system at a given time, and how it affected your ancestor.

Prison records

If your ancestor was subsequently sent to prison, you have several avenues to explore, including prison registers and calendar of prisoners, with the latter giving details of the person convicted, the name of the magistrate, the offence, details of the trial and finally, the sentence.

Prisoner no. 2517 (unnamed) at Wakefield prison, 1869, with a warder standing behind.
(© Wellcome Collection, public domain mark)

Most of the main genealogy websites have these records, and there is a blog from Birmingham Library on using the Calendar of Prisoners on Ancestry: **https://theironroom.wordpress.com/2020/05/28/how-to-use-the-calendars-of-prisoners-on-ancestry/**.

You can go deeper into the topic if your ancestor was sent to prison and there are plenty of online resources to help you do so. Prison History at **www.prisonhistory.org** lists seventy-eight Yorkshire places, from local prisons and lock-ups, through to city prisons. Each is linked to a modern-day map so that you can see the current building if applicable, or at least the place where it stood, and many of the listings also include dates of operation. Whilst the details are sparse on some of the entries, most have links to both primary and secondary sources.

Chapter 6

LEISURE AND RELIGION

In this chapter, we take a look at life outside the workplace, in the fields of leisure and religion. How our ancestors spent their leisure time, including at a place of worship if applicable can not only tell us what they were like as people, but also give an insight into their living conditions and surroundings, disposable income, their social circle and even their level of fitness.

Leisure
Before the start of the nineteenth century, organised leisure pursuits were largely confined to the upper classes, simply because it was only they who had the time and money for anything beyond concentrating on keeping a roof over their head and food on the table. However, with the move towards a more organised and urbanised culture, towns and cities began to expand their leisure offerings. As Shane Jessop explains in his excellent blog The Pursuit of Leisure and Sport in East Yorkshire (**https://shanejessp.wordpress.com/2015/05/31/the-persuite-of-leisure-sport-in-east-yorkshire-c-1850-1950/**) it was the coming of the railways that helped bring about a type of leisure time that was separate from home life, offering the prospect of day trips and holidays. With the first ever bank holiday implemented as a result of the Bank Holidays Act of 1871, the way was paved for the fun to start.

Between the two world wars, the influence of progressions such as the increase of Scarborough to Whitby trains in the 1930s saw people take to coastal towns for the day or longer, and this was also the decade of the Holidays With Pay Act. Finally, it was time to forget about work and home for a week and literally get away from it all, as the colourful – and often humorous – greetings from the heyday of postcards show.

The heyday of postcards in the 1930s–1960s. (© Tuck DB Postcards)

The Thoresby Society **www.thoresby.org.uk/** has a strong collection of digitised volumes that cover pastimes, hobbies and entertainment. The publications section of the home page (on the left-hand side) is where you can browse digitised volumes that can then either be purchased or read at **http://archive.org**. You can search by the general alphabetical index, contributors index or publications index. Some examples of the topics include 'Knowing One's Place' by Robin Pearson, which covers alcohol, the Armley Feast, art exhibitions, seaside excursions and musical performances.

One of the earliest of these records is 'bell ringing in Leeds' from 1632, a fascinating note written by historian Ralph Thoresby remarking upon the 'disorderly and much ringing' of the bells at Leeds Church, following which it was decided in a general meeting of aldermen, burgesses and assistants, that the ringing of bells following a funeral was to be controlled more closely, to avoid bell ringers creating a cacophony of noise for 'nothing else but their own pleasure and profits'. Henceforth, only the 'little bell' was to be tolled free of charge; anyone requiring the 'great bell' was to pay for the privilege.

Theatre and amateur dramatics
A trip to the theatre was an affordable treat for most and whether your ancestor was a performer, worked behind the scenes, or was an audience member, you can really bring the experience to life for yourself by combining several sources from the playbill and theatre programme collections below.

Leodis **www.leodis.net** is an excellent resource for West Yorkshire theatre history, with digitised playbills to explore that cover more than two centuries of theatre-going, from the 1780s through to the 1990s. Playbills not only give you an insight into the types of shows that were popular at a given time, but many also list the actors and actresses involved.

Playbills and programmes mention the names of performers and when it comes to well-known actors and singers, you can do an online search for more about his or her career and some may be featured on postcards, such as those at Tuck DB Postcards **https://tuckdbpostcards.org**. In the first decades of the twentieth century, there was a real craze for postcards of music hall actresses, with these Edwardian beauties posing with theatrical props such as umbrella or bouquet of flowers. These staged shots were the forerunners of photographs later issued on behalf of picture houses and featured in some of the numerous movie magazines.

A playbill or programme will have other information to follow up, such as the name of the theatre – which you can research – and its location; what other businesses operated on this street? Might theatre-goers have had restaurants or inns to visit nearby afterwards? As the years went on, some of these businesses would have placed advertisements in the programme. Next, you can search newspaper reports for the days before and after the performance, looking at reviews of the performers, how the performance was received by the audience, where the play was travelling to next, and so on.

You can get started at Leodis in the advanced search **www.leodis.net/AdvancedSearch** by selecting 'playbills' in the 'select a media archive' at the top left. From here you can browse by decade, theatre, year and collection (the repository). So, for example, selecting the turn of the nineteenth century – the 1800s, brings up forty-five different plays, including *Hamlet*, *John Bull* and *The Wags of Windsor*. Fast forward half a century and we have more than 300 plays to explore and have moved on from a simple sheet of paper that lists the actors and actresses, to a wider variety of Leeds theatres and much more dramatic and effusive descriptions of the people and plays involved. Clearly, promoters had to work much harder in the fact of competition from other theatres and alternative entertainments, such as a show staged on 15 May 1854, when theatre-goers were treated to a circus extravaganza with 'dancing-flying men', highly trained steeds and gymnastic heroes. The 'unequalled as a female artiste', Miss Emily Jane Wells, leapt garlands, rode backwards on a horse and performed 'feats unparalleled, whilst Signor Christoff

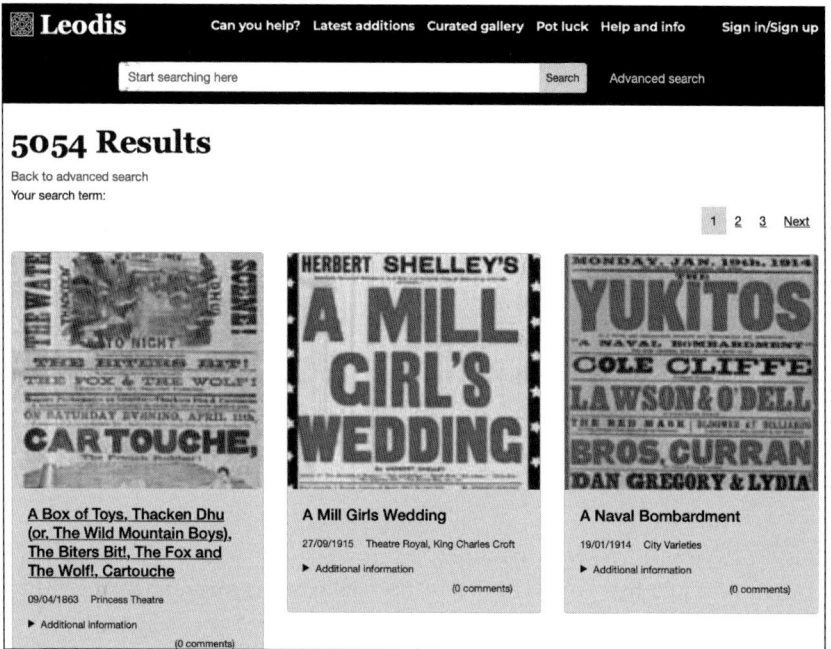

More than 5,000 playbills can be explored at Leodis.

displayed his own horsemanship on the 'cord of tension'. Boxes, pits and gallery seats were on offer, with prices ranging from 3d to 1s.

In a similar vein, Picture Sheffield has thousands of digitised items to explore. Again, use the advanced search option **www.picturesheffield.com/advanced.php** so that you can search by decade.

North and East Yorkshire have a rich theatrical tradition that focuses particularly on the seaside resorts and the entertainment they offered to both locals and holidaymakers. The Early English Drama project is a great way to explore the earliest years of the performance tradition. Reed Online **https://ereed.library.utoronto.ca** is the home of this database, and incredibly, the records covered date back to the year AD 680 with the Venerable Bede's account of a musical performance by Whitby Abbey inhabitant Caedmon.

Shopping

As you might imagine, newspapers and street/trade directories are a rich resource for information on businesses, the goods that they sold and the people who ran them and were employed there. Adverts are such an interesting way to get a snapshot of a locality or society at a particular point in time: the strictures of wartime and rationing; the blossoming of department stores and luxury goods; and the growth in time-saving products for those going out to work.

If your ancestor was a shopkeeper or commercial trader, you might well find him or her listed in a trade directory, perhaps along with an advertisement in the directory, or a newspaper, advertising their wares. Shop workers are less likely to have made it on to a written record, because of the often informal nature of the work. Larger concerns such as department stores may have staff records, in-house magazines and perhaps even photographs that may have been deposited either within the company archive, or at the local or county record office.

Maps, too, can give you an idea of the retail options that were available to your ancestor. Did he or she live within walking distance of a busy high street, or were they miles from the nearest shops? If so, how might they have reached their local shopping facilities? Street directories could give you an idea of how often public transport ran, which days town or village markets were held, and even which businesses offered local deliveries.

The National Media Museum in Bradford has a world-class archive and photography collection **www.scienceandmediamuseum.org.uk/researchers/access-to-our-collection,** with thousands of images available online. These include evocative photos of shops and shoppers over the decades. In 1964, the first 'moving pavement' in a British shopping centre opened at the Merrion Centre in Leeds, and a charming photo showing American jazz singer Joy Marshall trying out the pavement, which had cost £10,000, is available at **https://collection.sciencemuseumgroup.org.uk/objects/co8223367/the-first-moving-pavement-in-a-shopping-centre-leeds-gelatin-silver-print-photograph.** Explore the collections for photos of shops and memorabilia relating to your chosen town – the market photos are particularly evocative, capturing both stall holders and their wares, and shoppers of all ages.

Clubs and societies

As our ancestors gained more leisure time, the natural inclination of the human race to find those with similar outlook and interests came into play with the introduction of clubs and societies devoted to various pursuits. Such groups can be a surprisingly fruitful resource as to where you can find material, it tends to be very name- and information-rich.

Local newspapers often carry advance notices of club meetings, followed by sometimes quite detailed reports of the get-together. Prize-givings, performances, parties and visits from special guests could all merit a mention in print. And of course, many clubs had their own journals and newsletters, some of which have been digitised. Many clubs also kept record books of their annual general meetings, attendees at regular meetings, activities undertaken and so on.

If you're interested in a specific group which still exists, it's worth e-mailing the club secretary to ask about the possible whereabouts of the club or society archives – you may strike lucky and either be granted access if these are held by the group, or alternatively they may have been lodged with a record office and, if you're lucky, digitised.

Sports
Whether as a player or spectator, chances are your that your forebears had at least some involvement in sports, even if only during their school days. As you'd expect, newspapers are a good source of match reports, player awards, sports society activities, etc. However, there are other possibilities too.

The Yorkshire and Humber section of Sporting Heritage **www.sportingheritage.org.uk/content/collections/collections/england-directory/yorkshire-and-the-humber-england-directory** has more than twenty ideas for researching sport history, including the Dewsbury Memories online museum of the town's sporting heroes and heroines, the photographic collections of the National Media Museum in Bradford, and the University of Sheffield's online database of the UK's sports statues, dozens of which are in Yorkshire, covering over 1,000 statues nationwide.

The pride and passion of sport lends itself to the medium of film and this is where the collections at Yorkshire Film Archive come into their own. From a walking race in 1930s York, to wheelchair racing in 1970s Sheffield, there are hundreds of short films to choose from, many of which incorporate oral history by featuring interviews with sportsmen and sportswomen. If you have a fairly specific search parameter it's also worth trying a search on YouTube as there are many older gems there too.

Your ancestor need not have been a professional sports player; many people enjoyed playing in a school or work team. In the golden age of textiles, from the late nineteenth century through to the 1930s, many mills had amateur leagues that played other local teams. The Lister Ladies in Bradford, established in 1921, followed in the footsteps of the slightly earlier and very successful Dick Kerr Ladies, from the munitions' factory of the same name in Preston, Lancashire. Among their rivals were Hey and Company ladies' team, employees of a Leeds brewery. At this stage, women's football was still seen as something as a novelty, and had been a means of raising money during the First World War. Furthermore, the Football Association's ban on women's football in 1921 further cemented its reputation as an amateur-only sport in the decades that followed.

Adult education
The Victorian era heralded the start of the chance for the working man – and in due course, woman – to access education outside the childhood schoolroom. And for many, school attendance would been short, with the leaving age for boys and girls raised to 11 in 1893, to age 12 six years later, 14 by the end of the First World War, and then after several decades, a move to age 15 in 1947 and finally, 16 in 1972.

The British Newspaper Archive is a rich source of material here, **www.britishnewspaperarchive.co.uk** with fascinating accounts of people advertising for evening-class pupils. On 8 October 1870, the *Dewsbury Chronicle* informed readers that a Mr Bentley begged to announce that his evening classes were to resume, aimed at all young men who wished for 'general improvement' in the study of 'any particular branch of education'. The *Huddersfield Chronicle* of 29 May 1858 reported on the growing number of female participants at classes run by the Yorkshire Union of Mechanics Institutes, with classes at Marsden, Pudsey and Otley, such classes by the union being 'the only institutes exclusively devoted to the instruction of females in this country'.

Holiday week
Wakes week was a tradition that began in the mill towns of Lancashire and spread across England and Wales. Workers in a town would all be given the same week off work, with mills closed for the same seven days, meaning that workmates and neighbours could head off on holiday together, or bump into people they knew whilst strolling down the prom on the east or west coast. Usually neighbouring towns had their wakes week at a different time, to avoid overcrowding holiday hotspots. Scarborough, Blackpool and Filey were among the most popular destinations, but people were also prepared to travel further, to Scotland, Cornwall and the Isle of Man. This two-minute 1940s film on YouTube from Huntley Film Archives captures the excitement of cramming on to the train, the race to find a good spot on the beach at Blackpool, donkey rides, sandcastles and the funfair: **www.youtube.com/watch?v=GwJnV1rLne0**

Postcard and vintage postcard sites are another resource here, with sites such as Francis Frith, Tuck DB Postcards and even eBay providing black & white and colour images of popular seaside resorts and inland attractions such as Bolton Abbey in North Yorkshire and the West Yorkshire spa town Ilkley. The postcards of different eras give a flavour of changing attitudes towards holidays, from the genteel promenading of the Victorian era, through the more active pastimes enjoyed in the

Bridlington crowds, c.1912. (© Tuck DB Postcards)

Edwardian era with cycling and boating, and on to the cheeky and cheerful postcards sent between the two world wars, a decade or two before Brits began to experience overseas travel through package holidays.

Religion

Whether you're searching for Church of England or Nonconformist ancestors, the Genuki Churches Directory is a great first stop: **www.genuki.org.uk/churchdb**. Here, you can find the approximate location of all parishes that have existed since 1837, as well as a listing of all present and past church buildings, thus allowing you to move on to find out what genealogical resources are available where. Type in a place name, choose the county, and then click 'search' to see a map of all churches within a certain radius – the colour-coded pins each relate to a different religion. The listings vary in the amount of detail and so luck plays a part to some extent, but if you stumble across one of the more comprehensive entries it will have a photo of the church, the date of its foundation and of the earliest surviving records. Being able to see both present-day and former churches on one map is interesting and helpful for research too.

Next, use FamilySearch England Church Records Wiki **www.familysearch.org/en/wiki/England_Church_Records** to find the page for your parish of interest. Each of these pages will bring you to a table of online collections of Church of England records, as shown here, the dates for which records exist in the cases of baptisms, marriages and burials,

South Cave Online Parish Records

Collections	Baptisms		Marriages		Burials	
	Indexes and images	Indexes only	Indexes and images	Indexes only	Indexes and images	Indexes only
FamilySearch Collections-East Riding	1500s-1900s	-	1500s-1900s	-	1500s-1900s	-
Parish Registers - FamilySearch Catalog	1500s-1900s	-	1500s-1900s	-	1500s-1900s	-
Bishop's Transcripts - FamilySearch Catalog	1700s-1800s	-	1700s-1800s	-	1700s-1800s	-
FreeREG	-	1500s-1900s	-	1500s-1900s	-	1500s-1900s
Findmypast-East Riding ($)	1500s-1900s	-	1500s-1900s	-	1500s-1900s	-
Findmypast Bishop's Transcripts-East Riding ($)	-	-	1600s-1800s	-	1600-1800s	-
Findmypast Banns-East Riding ($)	-	-	1500s-1900s	-	-	-
Findmypast Marriage Licences-East Riding ($)	-	-	-	1600s-1800s	-	-
Ancestry Marriage Bonds-East Riding ($)	-	-	1600s-1800s	-	-	-
Ancestry-England & Wales, Birth, Christening, Marriage and Death Indexes ($)	-	1500s-1900s 1500s-1900s	-	1500s-1900s 1500s-1900s	-	1500s-1900s
Databases with Known Incomplete Parish Coverage						
Boyd's Marriage Indexes-FMP (Free)	-	-	-	1500s-1800s	-	-
National Burial Index-FMP (Free)	-	-	-	-	-	1700s-1800s

Find your parish of interest on FamilySearch England Church Records Wiki for an overview of what's available where.

and whether or not there is a charge to access the material. The same applies for Nonconformist church records, with its hub page at **www.familysearch.org/en/wiki/England_Nonconformist_Church_Records**

Church of England

The key records created by the Church of England (C of E), as far as family historians are concerned, are of course parish registers, as we saw in Chapter 2. But beyond this mammoth genealogy resource, the Church of England has many other resources to offer. It's worth bearing in mind that, no matter what religion our ancestors belonged to, they were nominally members of the Church of England in as far as all members of a community (usually with exemption of Jews and Quakers) were required to go through the process of baptism, marriage and burial through the auspices of the Church of England until the creation of civil registration in 1837. So, whilst you may find your relatives being baptised, wed or buried at a Church of England church, don't make the mistake of assuming they followed the state religion – the Church of England was *de facto* registrar of these life events, even if they were also (in the case of births and marriages at least) carried out elsewhere.

Was your ancestor a member of the C of E clergy? The Lambeth Palace research guide Biological Sources for Anglican Clergy **https://bit.ly/3g8T70i** is a valuable resource, full of suggestions for further reading, online databases, links to clerical directories and periodicals, plus information on those clergymen sent to work overseas.

Nonconformist

If your ancestor was a Nonconformist who reached the leadership ranks, he may have been educated at one of the dozens of dissenting academies around England, of which Yorkshire had at least four (Attercliffe, South Yorkshire; Heckmondwike, West Yorkshire; Rathmell, North Yorkshire and migratory). These institutions offered a vocational education to those training as a minister of religion outside the auspices of the Church of England from the time of the Reformation through to the late eighteenth century.

Dissenting Academies Online **https://dissacad.english.qmul.ac.uk** is a database and an encyclopaedia covering the years 1660 to 1860. It includes accounts of each academy, biographies of leading figures, and biographical data for around 11,000 students. It also includes suggestions for further reading. You can browse alphabetically, by student or tutor name, by academy, or by archive repository.

One example is Timothy Priestley (1734–1814), born in Birstall Field to Jonas Priestley and Mary (née Swift). Timothy was educated by James Scott, later a minister at Upper Chapel in Heckmondwike and he went on to become one of Scott's first pupils at his Heckmondwike academy. As well as undergoing a somewhat chequered career as a preacher, he also made electrical machinery to supplement his income.

Although some of the biographical information on the Dissenting Academies site is a little sparse, the further reading suggestions allow you to continue your study.

Dictionary of Methodism in Britain and Ireland **http://dmbi.online** is a similar encyclopaedic site, the online version of a book of the same name, first published in 2000 and now hosted on the Wesley Historical Society's website, with links to and from other Methodism sites. Among the highlights for those with Methodist ancestors are the town and village histories; biographies of individuals and of notable Methodist families; information on schools and colleges; and the Methodist stance on matters such as gambling, sex and alcohol. The town and village essays are a great way to get a feel for how Methodism became established in a particular district. In the case of Sheffield, this was a tumultuous start, with a mob encouraged by local magistrates destroying the first chapel in Pinstone Street just three years after its establishment in 1742. John Wesley opened the Norfolk Street Chapel in 1780 with other chapels and Wesley College following. The essay also includes notes from Wesley's diary, such as:

In the evening I preached at Sheffield, in the shell of the new house. All is peace here now, since the trial at York, at which the magistrates were sentenced to rebuild the house which the mob had pulled down. Surely the magistrate has been the minister of God to us for good! (April 1752).

Start at the help page **http://dmbi.online/index.php?do=app.help** to get a feel for how the site is laid out and then simply use 'search the dictionary' on the home page.

TheGenealogist is the official National Archives publisher for Nonconformism and has an introduction to these holdings at **www.thegenealogist.co.uk/non-conformist-records/**. These records go back to the mid-1600s, when those who refused to conform to the Church of England wished to worship in their own way. This huge online collection comprises over 8 million records, including what TheGenealogist calls 'hidden birth, marriage and death records' that can contain information spanning three generations of a family.

The BMD Registers **https://bmdregisters.co.uk** (£) has millions of Nonconformist records from The National Archives, which were deposited with the registrar general in 1841 (another collection was made in 1857). At the time of writing, viewing a page costs five credits (credits are 50p each) and you can also access these records on a subscription basis at TheGenealogist, Ancestry or Findmypast.

Roman Catholics

At Ancestry, Roman Catholic oath records for 1714–87, and 1829, contain lists and certificates of Roman Catholics failing to take the oaths of abjuration, allegiance and supremacy which were a part of an act passed by parliament in 1715: **www.ancestry.co.uk/search/collections/8632/**. Under this act, Roman Catholics were required to register their names and real estates with the Clerk of the Peace of the county where they owned property in order to attest to their loyalty. Those who refused to swear the oath were liable to be imprisoned.

The collection also includes an 1829 register of Roman Catholic Priests, gathered as a result of the passing of the Roman Catholic Relief Act by Parliament. Here, you can find details including name, age, residence place, residence date, and birth place.

The publications of the Catholic Record Society **www.crs.org.uk** are a real help in this area, especially with so many Roman Catholic records being available only on microfilm at archives and record offices. Founded in 1904, the society has published more than ninety works and its record series includes valuable transcripts of primary source material including diaries, letters, biographies, court and official papers.

Quakers

The Yorkshire Quaker Heritage Project, with its helpful guide is still very relevant to today's researcher. It is housed on the Hull History Centre website **www.hullhistorycentre.org.uk/research/research-guides/yorkshire-quaker-project.aspx** and was originally based at the Brynmor Jones University of Hull, in collaboration with the Borthwick Institute for Archives. The project undertook a survey of Quaker collections held by archives within Yorkshire (using the pre-1974 boundaries) as well as collections held elsewhere that relate to the region. You can access the resultant research guide – compiled by Helen E. Roberts and spanning a wide range of resources, both online and on site – at **www.hullhistorycentre.org.uk/research/research-guides/PDF/Researching-Yorkshire-Quaker-History.pdf**.

Nonconformist family history societies

Most of the Nonconformist faiths have their own family history or record society, namely:

- Baptism Historical Society **https://baptisthistory.org.uk**
- Catholic Family History Society **https://catholicfhs.online**
- Quaker Family History Society **https://newtrial.qfhs.co.uk**
- The Chapels Society **www.chapelssociety.org.uk**
- Unitarian Historical Society **www.unitarianhistory.org.uk**
- Wesley Historical Society **http://wesleyhistoricalsociety.org.uk/genealogy.html**

Non-Christian faiths

As so often, the FamilySearch Wiki is your friend here. For non-Christian ancestors in the post-civil registration period, your way of working should be similar to tracing ancestors who were Christians or not affiliated to any faith, as all births, marriages and deaths were recorded centrally.

For Yorkshire ancestors who you know were not members of the Christian faith during the era of parish records, be aware that your ancestors might still have 'ticked a box' by registering a life event in their nearest parish church, as well as undergoing a religious ceremony in their own faith.

Jews

The Jewish Genealogical Society of Great Britain provides unique resources: a library with more than 1,000 genealogy books to help you trace Jewish ancestors; a library of family trees; and numerous useful links to keep you abreast of the latest Jewish genealogy projects and updates. Learn more about the society at **www.jgsgb.org.uk/**.

Jewish Gen **www.jewishgen.org** is a specialist society for those with Jewish ancestors and has millions of searchable records, including 4 million relating to the Holocaust. There are also articles, a blog, a discussion group and Facebook group. The site also gives access to the Family Tree of the Jewish People, which comprises over 7.3 million individuals – either submit a Gedcom file or use the family tree creator at MyHeritage and import. MyHeritage is also a good place to search for Jewish records and you can find a good summary at **https://education.myheritage.com/article/how-to-research-your-jewish-ancestors-on-myheritage/**.

British Indian ancestors

Families in British India Society **https://www.fibis.org** help those whose ancestors lived in India – more than 3 million Britons across three and a half centuries.

Chapter 7

TRACING YOUR FEMALE ANCESTORS

Why a chapter specifically on tracing female ancestors? Simply because women can be harder to trace in historical records, but with a few tips, plus knowledge about where and how to look, you can reap rich rewards.

We'll take a look at the many records that specifically or mostly feature women, and also look at the case study of a remarkable Yorkshire woman who came from a very ordinary background, in order to demonstrate the types of records available and how these could be used on your own family tree.

Because the resources we've explored so far, such as birth, marriage and death records, the census and so on can be used equally for men and women, this chapter concentrates on those records that can be employed in addition to the widely used 'nuts and bolts' family history records that help us build our tree. Yorkshire has a wealth of female-oriented online resources – and an array of inspirational women mentioned within these – so let's dive in.

Why are women harder to trace?
As we soon realise when working on our family history, over the centuries the history of our country (and the wider world) has been written largely about men and by men. Of course, there are some exceptions, but the fact it is that it is generally harder to find our female ancestors on record. There are many reasons for this. For centuries, women carried out temporary work, or work that left little trace in the records. Many dipped in and out of work, fitting jobs in around family responsibilities. Add to this the fact that other places where we might expect to find a

Mary Shaw, a patient at the West Riding Lunatic Asylum, Wakefield. Photo attributed to James Crichton-Brown, 1871. (© Wellcome Collection, public domain mark)

record of our ancestors, such as clubs, societies and professional organisations, discouraged or did not allow women until well into the twentieth century. This may sound disheartening but knowing this information actually arms you with the facts so that you can take a different approach to finding your female ancestors.

And as a final incentive, I always find female ancestors the most exciting to trace because they are the ones that give you a new surname with each generation. Yes, it's great to follow your own surname down the centuries, but with each woman that joins the family along the way, you've been given a new surname to trace – and to potentially use to link up with others researching the same name.

Top tips for finding female ancestors

When using twentieth-century and earlier sources, remember that married women are often referred to in newspapers as 'Mrs [husband's first name] Surname', e.g. Mrs John Smith.

It sounds obvious but can be easy to forget – when searching records for a female ancestor's death and burial, remember that if the person was married at the time of death, you're looking for the person with their married surname – the name they would have been known by at the time they died – unless you have reason to believe they reverted back to their maiden name.

If you find an unusual middle name for one of a woman's children, this could be a clue to a father's surname if that father isn't named on birth records, or alternatively could be a way of keeping the maiden surname within the family. My great-grandfather Joseph Holroyd from Pontefract was registered in 1864 with the unusual middle name Burndrett. His parents' marriage showed his mother's surname was Burndrett and as a result of this clue, I've been able to trace the line back to a Thomas Brundred in 1770s Staffordshire.

What are the best sources for finding female ancestors?
For late nineteenth-century and early twentieth-century ancestors, the 1939 Register is a valuable resource. Because the 1931 census was lost in a fire, and the 1941 census not taken due to the war, this register is a valuable stepping stone from the 1921 census. It was taken on 29 September 1939 in order to produce wartime identity cards, but for our purposes, is perfect for identifying our female ancestors.

Although designed along similar lines to a regular English census, it gives exact date of birth (rather than year of birth on the normal census) exact address, marital status and occupation. And perhaps best of all, until 1991, it was updated with married name for those women who had been single at the time the register was taken, or with the new surname for those who changed name by deed poll. You can search the register online at Ancestry, Findmypast and TheGenealogist – any record of a person under 100 years old is not accessible unless a death has been proven and registered. See a great guide to the register from National Archives: **www.nationalarchives.gov.uk/help-with-your-research/research-guides/1939-register/**.

Rate books and the hearth tax (see Chapter 3) can also be surprisingly fruitful, particularly for single or widowed women, who would usually be classed as head of household for the hearth tax in this situation. However, both of these records do, by their nature, exclude poorer people – although you may find women listed in hearth tax exemption lists. For women of lesser financial means, and those who fell on hard times, more resources can be found below.

Poverty
As we saw in Chapter 5, ancestors who fell on hard times can leave their mark in various records and women – often with dependent children – who entered the workhouse would fall into this category. The first mention of this difficult life event might be finding an ancestor within an institution on the census; or perhaps if you don't find the woman concerned at the expected address, this could be a clue to widen your search to the hospitals and workhouses of the area.

In 2021, Ripon Workhouse Museum hosted an exhibition featuring five textile installations on the theme of women in the workhouse. Yorkshire-based textiles group, 6-Ply, created five installations that told stories based on historical research using the workhouse's records. Between 1901 and 1920, seventy-three babies were born at the workhouse, and many of these would have been illegitimate births. One of the installations paid tribute to Harriet Rodwell, who in 1855 committed suicide just three months after entering the workhouse. Her inquest revealed she had previously been held in a lunatic asylum but had shown no signs of insanity.

Ripon Museums were also involved in the More Than Oliver Twist project **https://riponmuseums.co.uk/workhouse-museum-garden/more-than-oliver-twist-project/**, which is a collection of pauper biographies researched by volunteers at six workhouse sites, including Ripon Workhouse Museum. One of the stories is that of Ann Hardbottle (*c*.1817–1889), researched by Mary Kelly, Ann was born around 1817 and appears on the 1841 census in Thirsk. Mary followed her through the censuses and notes how she spent most of her life caring for young and aged family members. By 1881, she was named as a seamstress at Ripon Workhouse and she died there in September 1889, with a report from the workhouse master noting: 'Ann Hardbottle, 70 years, a very patient sufferer who had been confined to her bed for many years died this night, admitted from the parish of Melmerby'.

Peter Higginbotham's workhouse site has an interesting essay on the type of work that female workhouse occupants would have carried out at **www.workhouses.org.uk/life/work.shtml**. Here, we read of women carrying out various tasks, which mostly seem to have centred around keeping the institution running. There were cleaning, laundry and kitchen chores, as well as outdoor work in the kitchen garden. Some women helped in the workhouse nursery, whilst others did mending and sewing.

Petitions and protests
One of the many ways our female ancestors can become visible in the records is when they were part of a campaign, protest or petition, particularly if they fell foul of the law in doing so and were thus named in a court action or even prison record. Of course, the suffragette movement of the first decades of the twentieth century is a great example of this, as we'll soon see.

Going back several centuries, Findmypast hosts the Quaker Women's Petition of 1659 **https://search.Findmypast.co.uk/search-world-records/quaker-womens-petition-1659?** which offers a rare glimpse of seventeenth-century women. More than 7,000 women signed this anti-tithe petition – not all of whom were Quakers. It is definitely worth checking with name and location if you've traced an ancestor back to the Early Modern period.

The British Library in London lists its online 'votes for women' digital resources at **www.bl.uk/votes-for-women** and this provides a useful introduction to the cause, with a timeline, research articles, scrapbooks, photographs and sound recordings, all of which can be accessed online. When it comes to finding an individual ancestor who may have been involved with the cause, as with other areas of family history, anyone who came to the attention of the authorities is more likely to have left a mark in the records – a 'quiet' protestor may leave no trace, a militant suffragette may be a different matter. The National Archives has records of over 1,300 women arrested for suffragette activism around England – recorded in the Home Office Index of Suffragettes Arrested. You can explore this on Ancestry (covering the years 1904 to 1914) at **www.ancestry.co.uk/search/collections/61005/**. You can also search the National Archives Discovery catalogue using keywords 'suffragist' and 'suffragette' or 'suffrag*' – suffragists were non-militant campaigners, suffragettes the militant arm of the cause and probably the better known nowadays.

Leeds-born suffragette Theresa Garnett pictured with fellow suffragette Annie Kenney in 1909. (Wikimedia Commons, public domain)

Findmypast's suffrage records include record series from The National Records and cover the years 1902 to 1919. Here, you can search for photos of suffragettes, explore calendars of prisoners and Home Office papers of suffragette disturbances, and see an official 'watch list' of 1,300 suffragettes covering the years 1906 to 1914. British Newspaper Archive and Findmypast have also digitised the newspaper *Votes for Women (1907–1917) and The Suffragette* newspaper, a weekly publication that announced the activities of suffragettes, upcoming meetings, and articles related to a wide range of women's issues. The paper had a circulation of 40,000 and this collection comprises newspapers from 1912 to 1918. When searching the records, try both maiden and (if applicable) married name, and also bear in mind that some suffrage campaigners used an alias, something which may only come to light through newspaper reports or court records.

The 1911 census is also a great way to discover an ancestor's link to the votes for women campaign, since some used this as a way to demonstrate their support, with the 'no vote, no census' slogan, fronted by campaigner Emmeline Pankhurst. She encouraged those in support of the cause to use the census taken on the night of 2 April 1911 as a way to mark their protest against the fact that women did not have the vote. There were several ways to do this, including spoiling the census form, being out of the house when the enumerator called, refusing to provide information on the form, or using the form to write a comment such as 'I am a woman and women do not count in the state'. Simply search the 1911 census in the usual manner to see if your ancestor, or someone in their household or neighbourhood, was involved.

Sheffield Libraries has a helpful digital guide **https://bit.ly/3NkkeBM** on tracing the involvement of women in various types of campaigning such as anti-slavery, anti-women workers' sentiment, and political campaigning. Although some of the information refers to material available at libraries and archives, it does include a useful timeline to women's protests, an introduction to the topics, and useful statistics on the percentage of women involved in politics or holding office at a particular time. There are also details of photos of groups and individuals involved in suffrage societies, which you can see online at Picture Sheffield: **www.picturesheffield.com**.

And finally, this East Riding Museums 'remarkable women' guide **www.eastridingmuseums.co.uk/EasySiteWeb/EasySite/StyleData/culture/downloads/museums/past-exhibits/beverley-guildhall/extraordinary-women.pdf** features dozens of influential women of the past in the fields of suffrage, charity, occupations and the arts.

Oral history

The Rowntree Society website **www.rowntreesociety.org.uk** explores the stories of workers at one of York's biggest past employers: the sweet makers Rowntree's. Founded by Joseph Rowntree in 1822 and initially run from a small grocery shop, the Rowntrees became a nationally famous family and a big employer. They had strong links to the Quaker faith – and acquired their cocoa business from a Quaker family named Tuke. You can read about the history of the company at the website noted below, which is also the home of the Rowntree Leisure interviews: **www.rowntreesociety.org.uk/video-projects/leisure-interviews/**. These short videos are based on material from the 1951 book *English Life and Leisure,* for which Benjamin Seebohm Rowntree was one of the interviewers. Despite its acknowledged lack of impartiality (explained on the website) it is a valuable snapshot into everyday life in the post-Second World War world.

Another collection linked to employment is the Nursing Registers of the Royal College of Nursing, which cover the years 1898 to 1968. These are located at Ancestry **www.ancestry.co.uk/search/collections/60423/** and comprise 1.5 million digitised records with (including maiden name, if applicable), nursing registration date and number. Additional details may include the home address, plus place and date of qualification. Prior to 1921, when the General Nursing Councils were established, different registers were kept, and this collection includes those. If you don't have an Ancestry subscription, you can apply to the Royal College of Nursing for a search of these Ancestry records using the form at **www.rcn.org.uk/library/archives/family-history** and this page also includes family history guidance, reasons that you might not find your nurse ancestor listed and ideas for other places to search.

Do remember when researching more recent, or more sensitive, history that some records will be subject to a 100-year closure period and/or you may be asked to prove your connection to the person whose record you wish to access.

Occupation clues

The Borthwick's guide **www.york.ac.uk/borthwick/holdings/research-guides/women/** features representative examples of the thousands of records they hold that cover women's lives from the thirteenth century through to the present day. Although the Borthwick is located in York, the reach of the collection goes far beyond the city walls.

Refreshingly, the Borthwick acknowledges that not only have women always worked, but that many females carried out a myriad of tasks at home as well as in the workplace – and there are digital collections that reflect this. This page **www.york.ac.uk/borthwick/holdings/research-guides/women/#tab-3** is a gateway to many collections and shows that records such as church courts and probate records may reveal an individual woman's records that wouldn't necessarily be recorded anywhere else, particularly for the years before the census.

As anyone who has tried to find an ancestor named in a company archive, very few company archives and records tend to name individuals, be they male or female, but you can find and use such records to research topics such as the pay gap between male and female employees, job descriptions, working conditions and more. Company magazines, too, can be of great use, particularly for industries such as textiles and banking, which employed large numbers of workers. The *Cocoa Works* magazine at the Borthwick has information on staff achievements and promotions, as well as more general industry news that might well have affected your ancestor and their community.

Ancestry has many women's service records, accessible via its card catalogue, the most recent of which (at the time of writing) is World

Flax pulling in Selby – Scottish English, Irish and Belgian farm workers with a male Japanese student at work in the fields. (© public domain)

War II Land Army Index Cards, covering the years 1939 to 1948. These employment records include name and address, dates of employment, age at enrolment, occupation and date of release. Because work on the land varied by season, you might find that an ancestor was employed in several different roles during the course of a year; because several records comprise several pages, be sure to look for an arrow at the right of the image to access multiple pages. There is also a bibliography at **www.ancestry.co.uk/search/collections/62020/** for reading suggestions if you'd like to explore the topic further.

Saltaire in West Yorkshire, a World Heritage Site, is also the home of the Saltaire Archive, which holds unique material relating to Titus Salt, the founder of village and Salts Mill. On the website **www.saltairecollection.org/portfolio-category/biographies/** you can find potted biographies of six women: Isabel Salt (1876–1968), Salt's only daughter; Dorothy Sharp, one of the founders of the Saltaire Historical Collection; and Harriet Byles, headmistress of Salts Girls' High School from 1886 to 1920; Medina Sarah Griffiiths (1840–1927) the first headmistress of the girls' school at Saltaire; Catherine Salt (1846–1930) a gifted singer who married Sir Titus Salt's youngest son – also named Titus, and finally Hannah Mitchell (1868–1936), the well-respected matron of Sir Titus Salt's Hospital. I found these biographies particularly interesting not only because of the life stories of these women but because, in many instances, we are shown where the material came from, e.g. newspaper reports, letters – giving ideas about further research on other women from our own families.

Although much of the Saltaire Archive is not accessible online, the website has online exhibitions, a searchable catalogue, and top level information for the Isabel Salt Collection – which can be explored from its home page at **https://bit.ly/424IZJw** from reports of speeches to Valentine's day party games, it is a fascinating glimpse into the lives of a group of privileged and socially responsible nineteenth-century Yorkshire woman.

Wills and obituaries

Even if your ancestor didn't make a will herself, she could well be named as witness or beneficiary on another will, so be sure to follow up a will where available for everyone on your tree. If your searches by name draw a blank, try searching for a will by place rather than name, as many people who might be mentioned in a will are not the testator, and so are not always indexed. If you do find a female ancestor named as a beneficiary of a friend, neighbour or family member, the relationship between the two people will usually be explained, which could put you on the path of other family remembers or more distant relatives.

Obituaries, often published in newspapers and society journals, can be genealogical gold dust as they can contain clues such as maiden name and place of birth, details of working life and also of hobbies, interests and charitable work outside of the home.

Case study: Florence White

As a Bradfordian myself, I couldn't resist including the story of campaigner Florence White. Born into an ordinary working-class household in Bradford, she became nationally known for her campaigning. As we'll see, the records that help to tell her story can also be used for our own 'everyday' female ancestors.

Born in 1886, Florence White was founder of The National Spinsters' Pensions Association in 1935, which grew to become a national campaign for married and single women. Florence and her compatriots campaigned for the age at which single women could retire to be lowered from 65 to 55.

We first find Florence mentioned on the 1891 census at Furnace Street, with her name spelt as 'Florance' – a reminder to try spelling variants if an initial search fails. The household comprises her Luton-born father James (born 1857), mother Caroline (born 1857 in Farnley) and siblings 10-year-old Albert and 1-year-old Annie. James may have been present on this census night but it was his regular absence from the family home, and the difficulties that this caused Caroline in caring for her young family, that inspired Florence in her later work.

By the time of the 1901 census, the family were still at Furnace Street but now Caroline was listed as head of household. Three of

First name(s)	Last name	Relationship	Marital status	Sex	Age	Birth year	Occupation	Birth place
Caroline	White	Head	Married	Female	44	1857	Stuff weaver	Farnley, Yorkshire, England
Albert E	White	Son	Single	Male	20	1881	Worsted spinner's clerk	Bowling, Yorkshire, England
Florence	White	Daughter	Single	Female	14	1887	Winder at worsted manuf	Bowling, Yorkshire, England
Annie	White	Daughter	-	Female	11	1890	-	Bowling, Yorkshire, England

By the time of the 1901 census, Caroline was listed as head of the four-person household.

the four occupants of the house were in the textile trade, with only 11-year-old Annie too young to work.

Florence became engaged in 1916 but sadly, like thousands of other women of her generation, her dreams of marriage were to be shattered when her fiancé died in France of pneumonia in 1917. She would never marry, and was to devote her life to the cause of promoting the rights of working single women.

We can next turn to newspaper reports on Findmypast to follow Florence's cause, beginning in 1935, when the *Leeds Mercury* of 28 May 1935 described her as campaigning to make Yorkshire and the rest of the north 'spinster conscious'. Interviewed in the living room above the Bradford bakery she owned, she spoke of her hopes that women would one day be able to draw their pension at age 55. In one single newspaper column we can read about Florence's home, workplace, the holiday from which she's just returned, and also hear her speak in her own words about her crusade.

The 1939 Register confirms Florence's date of birth as 11 June 1886, and here we have her living on Scholemoor Lane in Bradford with her sister Annie, who is listed as 'shop keeper, baker, grocer', and Florence given the occupation of 'hon secretary, organiser, Nat Spinster Pension Association'. From this information, it would now be possible to search for her birth certificate and from there, her parents' marriage record.

A further ten years' worth of newspaper articles follow, tracking Florence's campaign. The association disbanded in 1958 after twenty years of work from Florence and her fellow campaigners, who had achieved partial victory when the age at which single women could retire was lowered from 65 to 60. Florence died in 1961, just three years after the association had disbanded. Her funeral took place at Bowling Cemetery and her obituary in the *Telegraph & Argus* called her 'the champion of Britain's spinsters'. She is remembered on a blue plaque at Kirkgate, on Bradford's peace trail.

Chapter 8

EMIGRATION, IMMIGRATION AND 'STRAYS'

Emigrants landing at Lyttelton, New Zealand, in the 1870s. (© State Library Victoria)

Enrich your research by looking beyond the county to those record sets and organisations focused on both the Yorkshire diaspora (places in this country and overseas to which groups of people from the county have migrated), and Yorkshire 'strays' – people whose presence can be found in places you might not expect, which we'll explore in the second section of this chapter.

What can looking beyond the county offer you and your research prospects? Well, if your ancestors moved out of Yorkshire at some stage, you'll want to follow their story and it's helpful to be aware of resources that can help you do this. Also, as with emigrants from anywhere else in the world, many of our ancestors might have joined family, friends or neighbours and, at least in their early years in a new country, stuck close together and continued to celebrate the traditions and customs of home.

We'll explore both emigration and immigration in this chapter and for the purposes of both, it's important to remember that you should look for records in both the home country and the place to which the person emigrated. For example, if you have an ancestor who emigrated from Yorkshire to Pennsylvania in the US (a popular destination for textile workers) you might be tempted to concentrate on following that person's subsequent life in America. And, of course, your search will be rewarded by perhaps marriage records, the census and eventually a death record, but if you fail to continue your search in the original home country you could miss out. Local newspapers back home often carried letters, reports and obituaries for people who were well known in the community and had made a new life overseas. And the person concerned might have been named in a bequest from a friend or family member. Perhaps a search on the census at their old address might show other family members gradually following the original emigrant(s).

Strays

Having a knowledge of where to find Yorkshire strays can be a real help, particularly in those cases where you've 'lost' an ancestor between censuses who you believe should still have been alive, or in the case of a brick wall, where someone seems to have disappeared from your usual record sets.

What is a stray?

In family history, the term quite simply refers to a person who appears in a record set that is far removed from their place of birth or residence. Particularly in the days before online research and the useful digital indexes to the main databases we enjoy nowadays, helpful family historians would make a note of any strays they found out whilst carrying out their own research. These records would then be kept by a family history society, library or archive, for others to refer to.

Even now, with the many powerful search facilities of datasets at our fingertips, a strays' index can still be useful. After all, records can be mistranscribed, lost, and of course not be available online at all.

So, where to start? Genuki has a useful collection at **www.genuki.org.uk/big/eng/YKS/YRY/YKS/YKSCensusStrays** containing information that was extracted from a CD-ROM produced by the Church of Latter-day Saints. from the census returns for 1851 for the counties of Devon, Norfolk and Warwickshire. The information was then reformatted and sorted into alphabetical order by Carole Clyde. For the purposes of this database, a stray is defined as a person born in Yorkshire who appears in either the Devon, Norfolk or Warwickshire census in 1851. You can also find listings for Derbyshire, Lancashire, Lincolnshire, Middlesex, Northumberland and Surrey at the same link. In each case, the strays are listed in alphabetical order. Scroll further down the page for 1881 census strays in Wales. Each entry gives you surname, forename, relation to head of household, place of birth and date of birth. You can also search 'Yorkshire strays' from the home page of FamilySearch Wiki **www.familysearch.org/en/wiki/Main_Page**.

Many years ago, there was a National Strays' Index but according to a blog by Karen Kowalis at Lineage Tracer (**www.lineagetracer.com/articles/not-all-those-who-wander-are-lost-but-maybe-they-are-strays/**) this was discontinued around 2012, perhaps because it was felt that the growth of online indexes had rendered it less useful. This blog links to a strays' page on the British Genealogy forum **www.british-genealogy.com/forum/forums/448-Strays**, which is active and to which people are invited to submit any strays they find. Although the names are not listed alphabetically, there is an option to search 'forum only' with a keyword.

If you have an idea of the general area in which you might find your stray, it's worth contacting both the family history society and the county and/or local archive that cover that town or district and asking whether they have a strays' index or database. Failing that, try a web search with the first name, surname and the words 'stray' and 'family history' – you might strike it lucky and find the relevant person mentioned in an online index or on a forum.

Finally, an eighty-three-page booklet *Strays* by Beatrice Scott, published by *Yorkshire Archaeological Journal* in 1983 is available from second-hand online booksellers, and from Amazon.

Immigration

For centuries, Yorkshire has been known of a place of plentiful employment, particularly since from the beginning of the Industrial Revolution when the introduction of steam-powered mechanisation saw mills, mines and steel works become three of the county's biggest employers. Although, of course, people have come and gone for thousands of years, broadly speaking there have been three major waves of immigration to the UK: sixteenth-century incomers from France and the Low Countries; immigration triggered by the employment opportunities created by the Industrial Revolution from the late eighteenth century onwards; and finally, movement triggered by the two world wars, with new arrivals from Commonwealth countries.

Many of us will have immigrant ancestors within our fairly recent past and whether you've found out perhaps by a DNA test, old family stories, or traditional records that reveal place of birth, such as the census, there is plenty more that you can find out online. Within this section we'll take a look both at people who moved to the UK, as well as those who moved to Yorkshire from elsewhere around the country. When I first began to research my family history I was guilty, like many other people, of believing that communities of the past were fairly settled and that it was unusual for someone to move from their birthplace. I soon realised how very wrong I was – I knew that I had Irish ancestors, but I've also discovered forebears who arrived in the county from the south of England on a poor law rural relief scheme (as mentioned in Chapter 7), and others who have migrated south from Scotland, transferring their skills in the textile trade to the mill towns of Yorkshire.

There are so many countries from which people could emigrate to Yorkshire and so for the purposes of this section I've concentrated on migration from around the UK, and also from key countries overseas, as the main principles used here would also work for other countries, and also hopefully act as a springboard for further research. To get started, the National Archives has a really helpful introduction at **www.nationalarchives.gov.uk/help-with-your-research/research-guides/immigration/** which includes alien records, records of internees in both world wars, and records of naturalisation. Whilst not all of these are available online, many have been digitised and this guide provides a really good overview of what does – and doesn't – exist when it comes to exploring immigration as it relates to family history, and where the various records are held. As you read through, it soon becomes apparent that not only are most of the available records available only to search in person at an archive, but also that many potentially useful records are subject to a closure period.

The exceptions to the rule are The National Archives' incoming passenger lists (BT26) at Ancestry for people who arrived by sea from outside of Europe, and also record collections HO2 and HO3 for certificates of alien arrivals and returns and papers respectively, again at Ancestry.

The FamilySearch Wiki England and Immigration page **www.familysearch.org/en/wiki/England_Emigration_and_Immigration** is of similar assistance, with websites, indexes, images, e-books and databases, all organised under different sections relating to either emigration or immigration.

What records can I use?
Wherever in the country or world your ancestors migrated from, chances are that they probably settled in an area already peopled by others from their region or country of origin. This was the lot of the migrant – often being forced to take accommodation in the least desirable area of town, and work their way up.

All of the main genealogy subscription websites hold immigration records, which become richer in detail the newer they are. You can use the card catalogue or index to locate these collections and then use your ancestor's name and any details you know to start your search. Bear in mind that you may need to be open minded with your name searches as many people changed or tweaked their surname once they'd settled in a country, in order to fit in or avoid discrimination. Work backwards from the newest UK record of your ancestor that you have and be prepared to find a few name changes along the way. Unusual and non-native forenames and surnames are also more likely to have been mis-transcribed, either at source, or when digitised – try phonetic searches too, in case the name was noted down in the way it was pronounced, rather than correctly spelt.

One growing online resource worth checking periodically is the Immigrant Ancestor Project from Brigham Young University in Utah, USA: **http://immigrants.byu.edu/main_page**. This work in progress involves researchers using emigration registers to locate information about the birthplace of immigrants in their home country – information that wasn't recorded in port registers and naturalisation documents at the immigrant's destination.

The census
From 1841 onwards, the census is a great way not only to get a clue to place or country of origin but also to allow you to explore the ethnic make-up of the street or district where your ancestor settled. See Chapter 3 for more guidance on using the census, but for the purposes of this section, its value lies in exploring the houses and streets around the place where your find your forebears. Look at other neighbouring households – do the inhabitants also hail from the same place? You

Your search	Clear All	7 results						
First name(s)		Last name	First name(s)	Year Of Birth	Year Of Death	Year	Record set	Location
e.g. Winston ✕		Delander	Anastasia	1822	–	1891	1891 England, Wales & Scotland Census	Horton, Bradford, Yorkshire & Yorkshire (West Riding), England
☑ Include name variants		Delander	Bartholomew	1841	–	1891	1891 England, Wales & Scotland Census	Horton, Bradford, Yorkshire & Yorkshire (West Riding), England
Last name								
Delander ✕		Delander	Bartholomew	1869	–	1891	1891 England, Wales & Scotland Census	Horton, Bradford, Yorkshire & Yorkshire (West Riding), England
☐ Include name variants								
Year Of Birth	Give or take	Delander	Joseph	1872	–	1891	1891 England, Wales & Scotland Census	Horton, Bradford, Yorkshire & Yorkshire (West Riding), England
e.g. 1874	± 2yrs ✕							
Year Of Death	Give or take	Delander	Margaret	1878	–	1891	1891 England, Wales & Scotland Census	Horton, Bradford, Yorkshire & Yorkshire (West Riding), England
e.g. 1965	± 2yrs ✕							
Year	Give or take	Delander	Patrick	1875	–	1891	1891 England, Wales & Scotland Census	Horton, Bradford, Yorkshire & Yorkshire (West Riding), England
1891	± 0yrs ✕							
Location		Delander	William	1867	–	1891	1891 England, Wales & Scotland Census	Horton, Bradford, Yorkshire & Yorkshire (West Riding), England
Yorkshire, England								

The Delanders on the 1891 census in Bradford. An advanced search shows the family surrounded by other groups from southern Ireland.

might even be fortunate to find other family members living close by. For an unusual surname, or one that is associated with a particular country, try performing a surname search on that name and Yorkshire, to see whether others settled.

In the example shown here, I can see that my Delander ancestors are the only ones living in Yorkshire at this time. Fast forward ten and twenty years and it's still just those same key families. However, by using 'advanced search' on Findmypast, (or on Ancestry as shown on the support page here **https://support.ancestry.com/s/article/Searching-by-Location?language=en_US**) I can see that the Delanders have many southern Irish families living around them, most in textile-related occupations.

Family Tree magazine has a useful blog at **www.family-tree.co.uk/how-to-guides/why-cant-i-find-my-ancestor-on-the-census/** offering ideas on what to do if you can't find an ancestor on the census – ideas include considering whether the person could be visiting family, and checking for lost portions of the census.

Settlement records
These records are available on Ancestry, and for West Yorkshire cover the years 1689 to 1866. As shown in more detail in Chapter 5, they relate to the poor law of 1601 and the fact that parishes were required to care for the poor who had been born in their area. If someone moved to a new parish, perhaps from outside the county in question, should they fall upon hard times, the overseers of the poor would be keen to have the person concerned return to their home parish to claim that aid, hence the

existence of settlement certificates and removal orders. If you're lucky enough to find an ancestor in these records, the information can include current and former place and date of residence, details of spouse and children, professional information such as apprenticeship details, and information on other family members and their residence.

Records at Yorkshire libraries and archives
There are no immigration or emigration records unique to Yorkshire, and it can be difficult to find these records in digitised form in the catalogues of record offices, museums and libraries. UK GDL has a list of migration lists and records pertaining to Yorkshire here **www.ukgdl.org.uk/county/yorkshire/migrant_lists** and this also includes information on emigrants.

Ireland
According to a 2006 study by Owen Bowcott, around 10 per cent of people in the UK have Irish ancestry – and it is estimated that between 50 and 80 million people around the world have Irish roots, making this one of the largest diasporas. This importance is reflected in the existence of the Irish Family History Centre at the Epic Museum in Dublin, which offers an excellent on-site and online service. The museum tells the story of Irish immigration over the centuries and after a visit, anyone interested in finding out more is invited to visit the museum's family history centre. Here, you can book a personal consultation with a professional starting from €55 for thirty minutes: **https://epicchq.com/explore/irish-family-history-centre/**.

If you'd prefer to get started yourself, you can visit the hub page at **https://bit.ly/3T5eSww** to explore the many free resources, including a list of immigration resources around Ireland such as parish records at National Library of Ireland, the historical online maps at Public Record Office of Northern Ireland and its digitised copies of nineteenth-century street indexes to help you find an ancestor's location in their country of birth.

What was life like for immigrants in Yorkshire?
It's possible to gain an understanding of what it was like to arrive in England as an immigrant, and go on to build a new life. Newspaper reports, court records, oral histories and photographs can all play their part. The principles outlined in Chapter 10 apply here too – as maps, the census, postcards, photographs, film footage and so on can show you what life was like in a particular place at a given time. For immigrant-focused study, there are several possibilities.

The Saltaire Collection has a very interesting PDF on what life was like for migrant workers, particularly in the textile trade, in Bradford between the 1820s and 1967: **www.saltairecollection.org/wp-content/ uploads/Migrations-to-work-in-Bradford-1820-1970s.pdf**. The study looks at Irish, German and Eastern European waves of migration, finishing with Commonwealth migration.

The Making Histories website has a twenty-four-page collection of migration stories **https://bit.ly/44HujRd** and this includes tales of more recent immigrants from 2004 onwards, when Sheffield became the first UK city to take in resettled refugees.

Emigration

As with immigration, it's helpful to remember to search for records in both the home country and in the new country, for the rest of the person's life; links with the home country will usually remain and your ancestor could appear in a newspaper story, obituary column, will or collection of letters long after they emigrated.

Once again, there is no central database, online or otherwise, for tracing emigrant ancestors for any country, but, nevertheless, there is plenty of scope for adding flesh to the bones for this type of life event.

An overview

For a general introduction, section 4 of the National Archives guide at **www. nationalarchives.gov.uk/help-with-your-research/research-guides/ emigration/** outlines the online records available, which include outward passenger lists (1880–1960), early emigration records (1636–1815) and resources from the Immigrant Ancestors Project **http://immigrants.byu. edu**.

Sheffield Indexers have a superb hub page at **www.sheffieldindexers. com/Links/Links_EmigrationImmigrationMigration.html**, which leads to dozens of helpful resources including pre-1900 emigration records, Canadian war bridges, ship passenger lists, the 1881 census for ships in port listings and lots more. Don't miss the 'genealogy links by country' link so that you can dive into exploring the research possibilities for your country of interest.

Because it would be impossible to cover the records of every country, I've chosen some of the most popular emigration destinations of the last four centuries. As with immigration records, once you've established what material might be available, similar research principles would apply for any country.

Canada

Pier 21 is the Canadian Museum of Immigration and has a strong track record of helping people around the world whose ancestors emigrated to Canada and might well have passed through Pier 21, Canada's equivalent of Ellis Island. Its cited strengths are immigrants who arrived from Europe between 1928 and 1971; British Home Children and post-war displaced persons.

The Scotiabank Family History Centre at Pier 21 **https://pier21.ca/research/immigration-records-and-family-history** offers remote research services for people who are not able to visit the museum but would like to locate an immigration record. Staff use a variety of internal and external sources to locate immigration records, manifests and passenger lists. They can help with arrivals between 1863 and 1935, British war brides (Second World War), and anyone sailing from the UK before 1960. Online resources include a ship arrival database, passenger list database, and the facility to order an image of the ship on which your ancestor set sail – a great way to help you illustrate this milestone. You can also listen to oral histories at **https://5104.sydneyplus.com/final/portal.aspx**.

There are strong links between Nova Scotia and Yorkshire between the years 1772 and 1775, when around 1,000, mostly Yorkshire, migrants, many of them Wesleyan Methodists, resettled in Nova Scotia. The group was recruited by Nova Scotia's governor, Michael Franklin, who made the long journey to the north of England in 1771, in search of farmers to follow him back to Nova Scotia. The new arrivals settled mostly in New Brunswick, helping to establish the Methodist Church in Canada. This event was so significant that it has its own website: **www.libris.ca/yrkfam/**. Here, you'll find biographies, details of the various families compiled through passenger registers, letters and local histories. If you find an ancestor listed, you'll be pleased to find that many of these individual entries have a contact e-mail, meaning you could potentially connect with a distant cousin. As with all such databases, do treat the information with caution and verify independently – although this database provides a good starting point, some of the information comes from unverified or secondary sources; this is noted where applicable. If you're interested, you can also follow the 'further links' to research more of your Nova Scotia heritage.

USA

Like Canada, the USA has strong Yorkshire emigration links, some of which relates to the county's textile heritage. For millions of people,

Main Building on Ellis Island where 12 million immigrants to the US were processed between 1892 and 1954. (© David Brossard, CCASA 2.0)

the Statue of Liberty has symbolised the hope and prosperity that was anticipated when undergoing the daunting task of starting a new life in America.

Over the centuries, millions of emigrants have passed through the Ellis Island Centre in New York, now the home of the Ellis Island National Museum of Immigration **www.statueofliberty.org/ellis-island/national-immigration-museum/**, a place that tells the stories of the millions of people who passed through the centre, and whose descendants can now be found in all of the American states.

The museum has its own Family History Center, which houses a huge collection of immigration records, many of which are available online. Although you need only a name to get started, museum staff recommend that you gather a little more information before starting your search. So, if you know your ancestor's hometown, rough date of arrival, port of departure and even the names of any travel companions, you can make your search more precise. Some passenger records are more complete than others, but many reveal name, age, date of arrival, ship name, nationality, birthplace, occupation, last residence overseas and final destination.

Use the how-to videos and passenger search database downloadable PDF to help, from here **www.statueofliberty.org/discover/genealogy-primer/** and if you need more support, you can upgrade to 'voyage' level (£) to be teamed up with an Ellis Island research expert: **www.statueofliberty.org/support/become-a-member/**.

The Immigrant Servants database at Price Genealogy is another helpful, free database in which you could find your emigrant ancestors **https://immigrant.pricegen.com/login/login.php** as listed in Colonial American and European sources. The database aims to create a reconstructed arrival list for those who came to the US as indentured servants, redemptioners or transported convicts between the years 1607 and 1820. You can search by surname or place name and again, a research service (£) is offered.

If you know the geographical area from which your ancestor emigrated, it is worth a general web search, as you may have cousins in the US who share the same ancestors as you. For example, Howdenshire History **www.howdenshirehistory.co.uk/yorkshire-usa-emigration.html** has pages of resources for emigration to Canada, the US, Australia and 'worldwide'. The stories give a rich flavour not only of what resources can be put to good use in your search, but also of what life was like for those early emigrants. For generations after an emigration, there would have been families on either side of the ocean who were in communication

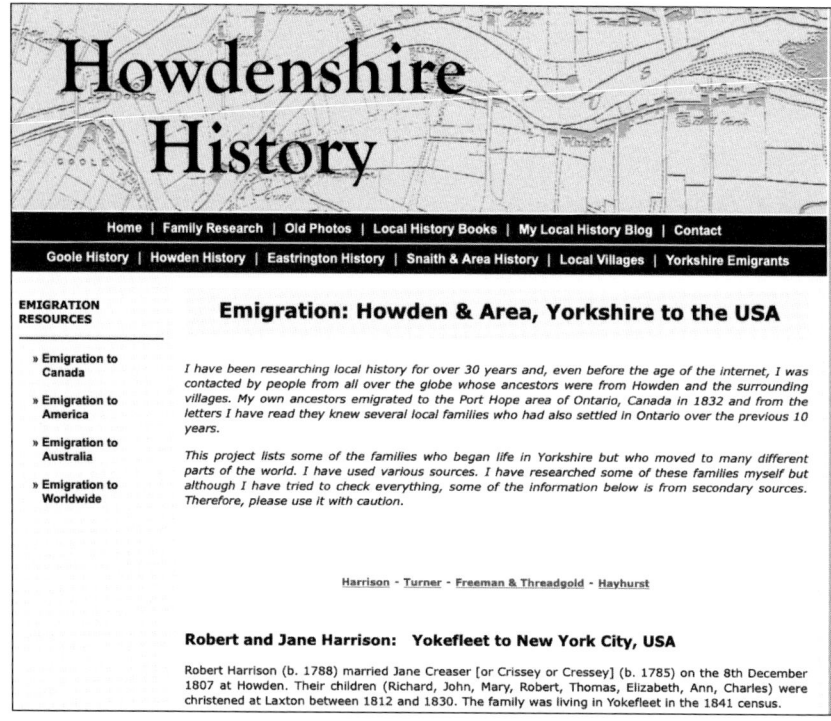

Howdenshire History is the result of three decades of research on immigration between Yorkshire and the US.

with each other – writing to brothers and sisters about their respective children, passing on news from their neighbourhood and commenting on the ups and downs of life.

Australia

For Australian ancestors, Trove Australia **https://trove.nla.gov.au** is the perfect starting point, whether your ancestors came here in the early days of emigration, or were among the 'ten pound Poms' who left the UK in the years following the Second World War. Here, you can browse newspapers for adverts for boats taking emigrants, places where passengers could go to book their tickets, as well as records relating to life in the person's new country, including notices of achievements and awards, and also obituaries. There are also diaries, letters, photographs and even recipes printed in Australian magazines, the latter reflecting strong ties to the home county. All the resources on the site are free to use, with comprehensive information on their original provenance.

The collections also include information on those people who didn't emigrate by choice – convicts. The study 'Yorkshire convicts who sailed on 2nd fleet to Australia' by M. Flynn includes fascinating biographies, as the following extract shows:

> Elizabeth Carter, late of Burton Pidsea, spinster, appeared at the 19 July 1788 Quarter Sessions for the East Riding of Yorkshire held at Beverley. She was charged with burgling the house of Robert Greaves, a hawker and peddler of Witherwick, stealing two silver crowns, two gold rings and various items of clothing valued at £10 ... She was sentenced to seven years' transportation. In late September she was one of five women sent from York to London for embarkation on the 'Neptune'.

Ireland

Just as many Irish have emigrated to England over the centuries, so too has travel flowed in the other direction. One of the best resources for those who emigrated to the north of Ireland is a 15,000-name database of census strays created by members of the North of Ireland Family History Society **www.nifhs.org/resources/miscellaneous-records/census-strays/**. This lists people found in the English censuses who were born in Ireland. For many of these records, additional information is provided, as well as the source of the record concerned and who recorded it.

Perhaps unsurprisingly, it is difficult to find online information for emigration in the direction of Ireland, maybe because of the huge Irish diaspora, meaning that more effort has been expended on this over the years. One key exception was the movement of British settlers to Ulster in the seventeenth century, as charted in an excellent paper by William Macafee, a member of the Ulster Historical Foundation guild, whose website hosts the text **www.ancestryireland.com/understanding-plantation/movement-of-british-settlers-into-ulster-during-the-17th-century/**. As well as explaining the background to the migration, we are also taken through the sources that can help us search for data.

Chapter 9

WORKING WITH OTHERS: SOCIETIES, SOCIAL NETWORKING AND VOLUNTEERING

In this chapter we'll take a look at the many ways in which you can work with others to expand and enhance your research, whether that's through helpdesks and forums, society talks and events, or volunteering your services. We'll also explore the possibilities and benefits of working with a professional researcher when you need help or advice, or even just a fresh pair of eyes on a research query.

Family History Societies
Soon after you start your family history research, chances are you'll come across reference to one or more family history societies. So much more than a group of like-minded individuals, these societies have members with deep knowledge of the area in question. Paying a small annual fee for membership will give you access to benefits such as meetings (many of which are on Zoom), a regular journal with articles about the area and its people in years gone by, and often the chance to take part in projects, and to benefit from the results of these through publications such as CDs and printed booklets. Keep a look out for 'surname interest' lists, as these can connect you efficiently to others researching the same line, particularly if it's an unusual surname, or one that is common in the area in question.

When it comes to family history societies for Yorkshire, unlike many other places around the UK, there are several different societies and groups that cover the whole of the county. A great place to start is the

Yorkshire Group of Family History Societies **https://yorksgroup.org.uk**, an umbrella organisation for the many societies that cover various areas within the pre-1974 three Ridings of Yorkshire. The parishes page **https://yorksgroup.org.uk/parishes-a-to-z-index/** is a useful alphabetical list that enables you to identify your parish of interest and find out which family history society covers that place. The societies section **https://yorksgroup.org.uk/societies/** covers some – but by no means all – Yorkshire societies, with web links and Facebook/Twitter pages where applicable.

You can find a much more comprehensive list at FamilySearch **www.familysearch.org/en/wiki/Yorkshire_Societies**, which begins with regional societies and then moves on to dozens of town and village family history and local history societies. For example, Bradford Family History Society explained how their online provision works:

> Details of our publications and meetings are all on our website **www.bradfordfhs.org.uk**, plus some Bradford Trade Directories (for everyone, not just members). For members there are more articles, our quarterly magazine and other society magazines that we have an exchange agreement with, such as Calderdale, Barnsley and Airedale, amongst others. We also offer members help with a small amount of research through our Link Scheme on an expenses-only arrangement. This may be a visit to Bradford Local Studies or West Yorkshire Archives (Bradford) to look at documents, newspapers or books. We also have a surname search facility, whereby members can see if anyone else is researching the same surnames. If so, they can send an e-mail to these members to get in touch.

Most recently, the society has been working on a database of searchable records for members. This is a Heritage Lottery funded project in conjunction with the City of Bradford Metropolitan with the initial batch of records being from the West Yorkshire Archives (Bradford). Bradford Poor Law Union Records (Ref: BU/6) are due to be released first.

When assessing family history societies, don't overlook those that have a 'foot' in Yorkshire, such as Cleveland Family History Society **https://clevelandfhs.org.uk,** whose area of interest incorporates a section of North Yorkshire.

And on the subject of being out of area, remember that you even if your ancestors don't hail from the area where you now live, it could well still be worth your while joining the family history society for your home town, if only for the social side of things when you want a change from online studies. And of course, the general family history advice that is a feature of society meetings and journals is not always restricted to a certain geographical area.

Yorkshire Roots **www.yorkshireroots.org.uk** is the family history section of the Yorkshire Archaeological Society and is based in Leeds. Founded in 1973, it has several hundred members around the world. Members benefit from monthly Zoom lectures (usually on a Saturday), a thrice-yearly journal *The Yorkshire Family Historian*, to which you can submit your research interests, and also access to a link scheme whereby volunteers may look up information from a library, record office or archive that you are unable to reach.

Society of Genealogists **www.sog.org.uk** is a nationwide organisation that boasts the 'UK's premier collection of family history records'. A recent addition to the membership benefits, and one that has caused excitement in the genealogy world, is the family trees collection **www.sog.org.uk/our-collections/family-trees/** which comprises digital images of hand-crafted historical trees. A work in progress that will eventually include 20,000 trees, each tree has been indexed and together, they contain over 1 million names – available exclusively to members.

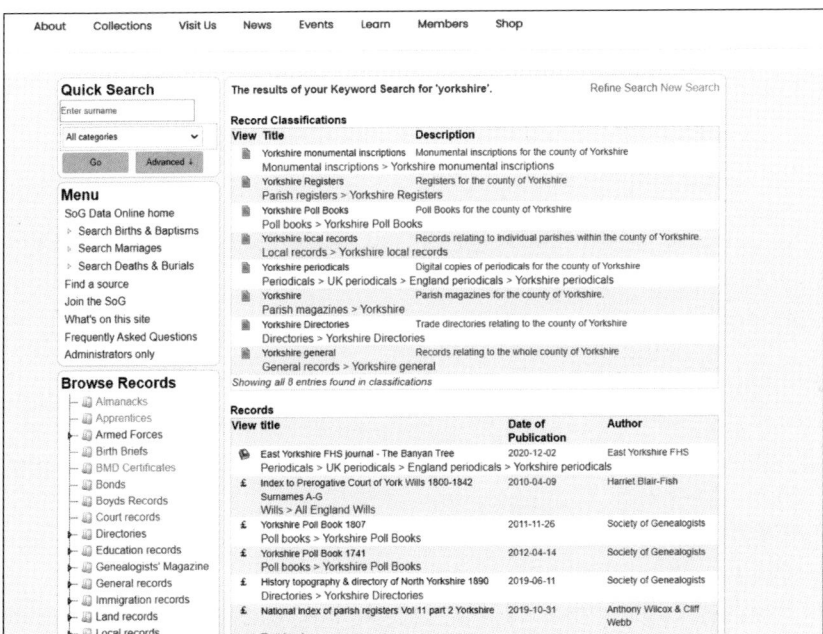

Society of Genealogists search page for Yorkshire.

Founded in 1911, the society has been helping genealogists for more than a century and has a growing number of records available online, with more being added. The society's library catalogue lists the useful books, CDs and micro media held in the library and you can find the catalogue at **https://s10312uk.eos-intl.eu/S10312UK/OPAC/Search/Browse.aspx**; from here, look for information the SoG holds on sources for parishes and places in Yorkshire, such as copies of original parish registers or memorial inscriptions. You can also search by subjects such as Yorkshire wills as well as searching by place.

Many of the SoG's compiled family histories relate to Yorkshire families so you can search the library catalogue for family histories relating to specific families (start searching by surname rather than individuals in the family). SoG is also working with FamilySearch to scan these family histories and some of these digital images will be available to members online in due course.

Else Churchill, genealogist at SoG, explained:

> We are starting a major digitisation and, for example, all our bound transcripts of parish registers and monumental inscriptions have been scanned and those which are our copyright or out of copyright will in due course be published online. We hope to start uploading to a new platform to host these items in 2023.
>
> We hope to follow this by scanning all our local directories and periodicals. A few Yorkshire directories were actually scanned and put online as a pilot project but there are more to add. All our poll books have been scanned and are already online and those for Yorkshire can be found amongst the online poll books in our digital collections. If you browse the online collections and look, for example, in the directories, poll books, local and parish register sections, you will find those Yorkshire books from the library that have already been scanned and uploaded.
>
> If you use the advanced search option **https://sogdata.org.uk/bin/aps_advanced_search.php** and put 'Yorkshire' into the keyword search box you will see some useful datasets and scanned books from the library relating to Yorkshire contained in the collections as shown below but this does miss those which didn't have Yorkshire in the title.

Local history societies can be extremely helpful when researching the surroundings of our ancestors, and their places in the communities where they lived and worked. British Association for Local History has

Yorkshire listings at **www.balh.org.uk/societies-az?county=YORKS** and as with family history societies, these groups offer meetings, publications, projects and, sometimes, help from volunteer members.

Steven Bruce of Yorkshire Family History advises:

> Make use of the collections and/or digitised data of any local family history society, local history society and/or record society covering the area of genealogical interest. Family history societies in particular have had to turn their attention from transcribing parish and census data. York Family History Society has a superb MI collection of many parish churchyards on CD or for download to include a photo of the gravestone as well as a full transcription. Also try Special Collections held by universities. I've recently located a will of a York resident from the 1630s whose will is deposited at Nottingham University Special Collections department.

Specialist Societies

If your interest is more specific, you can find guidance and connect with others via societies set up for a single research purpose, for example researching a particular surname, a DNA connection or a type of local history. One such example is the long-standing Thoresby Society **www.thoresby.org.uk**, which covers Leeds and district and was founded in 1889. Members enjoy Zoom lectures, and the website also has plenty of

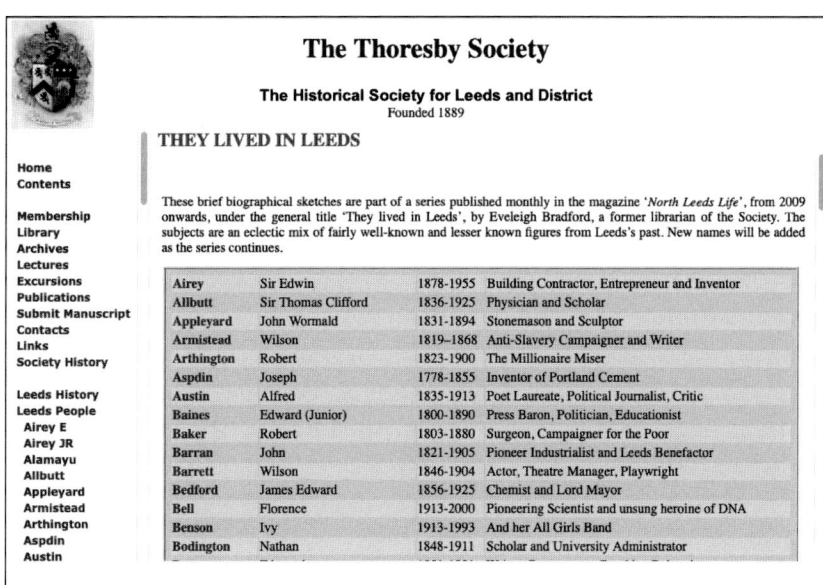

The Thoresby Society's 'they lived in Leeds' database.

free-to-access information including Leeds people, a Leeds dictionary, reading suggestions and access to scholarly articles housed at **archive.org**. Don't miss the 'they lived in Leeds' section **www.thoresby.org.uk/content/people/people.php** for mini biographies and pictures of Leeds dwellers from all walks of life.

If yours is a surname with a strong prevalence in Yorkshire, such as Lofthouse or Metcalfe, there may well be a surname society, or social media group dedicated to the study of that name. The Metcalfe Society **www.metcalfes-online.co.uk** caters for those with this surname and its variants and, like many other societies of its type, has published relevant material over the years which you can buy from the website. The society is currently working on a project to make its archives accessible online. On this same subject, the Guild of One-Name Studies has a Yorkshire regional meeting which, at the time of writing, is held online.

There are also societies that cover a particular trade or occupation and these can provide a refreshing slant on the topic, as well as access to material and knowledge that it would be difficult to find elsewhere. Another industry-related group is the South Yorkshire Industrial History Society **https://syihs.co.uk**, a charity that works to further the study, investigation, description and preservation of the historical and archaeological evidence of the trades that have been carried on in South Yorkshire from earliest times to the recent past. Although most of their events are held offline, they have a helpful web links section for further study on their website, details of interesting visitor sites connected to South Yorkshire's industrial past, plus an image gallery.

Other societies such as the Huguenot Society **www.huguenotsociety.org.uk/family-history.html** whilst not directly related to the county, can provide information that other online (and on-site) repositories don't possess.

And finally, if you've taken, or are considering, a DNA test for family history, your tests results – what is often called the raw data – can help you connect with others who have Yorkshire roots. Once you've undergone the expense of taking a DNA test, it usually costs you nothing more to upload your results to different sites and projects, although of course you should make sure you're happy with the terms and conditions, and double-check how your data will be used.

The Nidderdale DNA project is an excellent example of such a project **www.nidderdalednaproject.co.uk**. This group is building up a database of people who have a proven paper-trail connection to the Nidderdale area of North Yorkshire. Through the results, the project team hope to plot Nidderdale family movements into and out of the area and discover how many were in Nidderdale when parish records for the area began. Anyone who fits the bill is asked to upload their test results for free to FTDNA, which is the home of the project. Both male and female participants are welcome and the website has lots of links to Nidderdale family history, including headstone details, photographs, lineage information and statistics on surnames. As with other DNA projects, the more people who take part, the more accurate and helpful the results will be over time. You can use the surname and forename search to find out whether or not your name might already be under investigation.

FTDNA also has a Yorkshire project page **www.familytreedna.com/groups/yorkshire/dna-results**, which currently has over 275 members, with a map of group member locations, member haplogroups and SNP test results. Kirklees Cousins has an interesting 'who do you think you are?' section **https://kirkleescousins.co.uk/who-do-you-think-you-are/** and profiles four different Yorkshire DNA studies and projects, and also links to off-site resources: a genetic map of the UK and genetic cluster maps that you can explore with your Yorkshire roots in mind.

Connecting with Others

No matter how much we enjoy our research, family history can sometimes be a lonely pursuit, as many of us discovered during the Covid-19 lockdown. In this section we'll take a look at some of the many ways in which you can connect with others, including helpdesks and forums.

Genealogy forums can be great for those quirky, and often localised, questions you might have. Most of these are arranged around specific topics such as a particular surname, place or specialism, for example DNA or local history. Many have a Yorkshire page, and most will be able to offer advice on even quite specific queries, although the nature of forums does mean that your query might stay unanswered for quite a while.

Where to start with forums? If you're hoping for a timely response, look at a selection of sites and check when the most recent thread was posted and answered. If this was a few years ago, you might want to look elsewhere. A busy site will usually have the most engaged users. The Sheffield History genealogy forum **www.sheffieldrecordsonline.org.uk/cgi-bin/yabb2/YaBB.pl** is one such site, with many different topics including military, brick walls and a lookups section for offline records. Other interesting sites include RootsChat – one of the biggest sites for UK users **https://rootschat.com**, Family Tree Forum **www.familytreeforum.com** and Great War Forum **www.greatwarforum.org**.

Curious Fox **www.curiousfox.com** is another great site to bookmark. This covers the UK and Ireland and allows you to search or add a query by surname and place name. The maximum search radius is 10 miles around a particular town or village. The site is free to use at the basic level, which means you can add a query to the site but only paid members can contact you; if you're a paid member anyone can contact you.

In the last few years, social media has blossomed in terms of the support it can offer genealogists. Many archives, libraries, groups and societies have a presence on Facebook and/or Twitter, and these can be a great way to learn about record releases, upcoming and completed projects, events and volunteering opportunities.

Professional Research

Whether you've hit a seemingly insurmountable brick wall in your research, want help using an unfamiliar record set, or to benefit from specialist local knowledge, you may want to consider hiring a professional researcher. The assistance of a professional genealogist could save you hours of work, allow you to benefit from records you might not even realise exist, and will provide a fresh perspective on your ancestors.

So, what can a professional researcher do that you can't? Well, firstly the obvious, the right person would be trained and have many years of experience at solving genealogy problems. Even if you've been researching your tree for a long time, it's all too easy to get stuck in the habit of using the same record sets, or looking at a problem from one particular angle. By enlisting the help of a professional, you're allowing someone to take a look at the case afresh. Although you can ask a researcher to start a tree from scratch, many people hire them to tackle a particular ancestor or puzzle. Military or overseas records are just two of the areas of research where you might benefit from expertise in interpreting and accessing record sets. Or perhaps you've come across older records, written in Latin, and need help translating and interpreting these.

If your research is mainly online and you don't live in Yorkshire, then a professional who can access the records 'on the ground' in the county could be of huge benefit; they could visit county record offices on your behalf, call in at graveyards and smaller archives, all within the context of a deep knowledge of the county's history. In this case, hiring some help could actually save you money when you factor in the potential costs of a visit to the area yourself.

How do I choose a researcher?
As with any paid-for service, it pays to do your research, ask for recommendations, read reviews, and ask questions of the person you're considering hiring before committing yourself. The Register of Qualified Genealogists **www.qualifiedgenealogists.org** is a good place to start. Every genealogist featured on its website is a qualified professional who is registered with the organisation, and many undergo ongoing training to keep their skills up to date. These qualifications are from accredited institutions and have been taken at post-graduate level.

The 'find a QG' section sets out the various specialisms that a researcher may have and explains what this would mean in practical terms, e.g. someone listed as specialising in 'Sheffield' would be expert in the records of that city, or a person with expertise in palaeography would be skilled in reading and deciphering old handwriting. In 'genealogists profiles' you can browse the full selection or enter keyword and/or location.

Another great site is The Association of Genealogists and Researchers in Archives (AGRA), which has 'find a researcher' **www.agra.org.uk** where you can put in your geographical area of interest.

Of course, there are many experienced and extremely capable professional genealogists who are not members of either of the above; as you would when considering whether to employ any other professional,

Add keyword and/or location to find a professional researcher at the RQG website.

ask for recommendations, have an initial chat to see whether you could work well together and be upfront about what you are hoping to achieve and the avenues you've already tried.

What information should I provide?
Save yourself time and money and give your query a better chance of success by providing as much information as you've been able to gather, no matter how much or little that might be. Most genealogists charge by the hour and so if you can provide details of records you've already searched and drawn a blank, these can usually be eliminated from the enquiry.

The price you're quoted will depend on how many hours of research are involved, but the researcher should usually be able to give you at least a rough idea of the potential charge, or you can specify a maximum amount you wish to spend before the researcher comes back with a report.

Archives and helpdesks
County and local archives and libraries can often help with recommending professionals who regularly work with their materials, and many such institutions run regular in-person, telephone or online help desks, as do some family history societies. For example, East Yorkshire FHS not only has physical help desks at the society centre or a local library, but also offers online and e-mail help facilities where members can send in a question for the resident volunteer experts to look at. Society of Genealogists also offers a telephone service to its members, which is open for all genealogy questions.

> **Top tip from professional genealogist Anne Sherman**
> *Think outside the index*
> Just as not everything is on the internet, our ancestors' lives are not all indexed in databases. Many archive services and family history societies have access to books or projects that contain details of our ancestors but their names are not indexed.
>
> One example is the *Beverley East Yorkshire – Green's Household Almanack* dating from 1885–1953 in thirty-five books. These contain a local roll of honour with photographs of First and Second World War servicemen (not all of whom were killed), and advertisements for various Beverley businesses amongst other items: **https://bit.ly/3CgnGKu**. Most of the First World War servicemen in these

> books have been researched and their biographies have been added to the East Riding Archives website: **www.eastridingarchives.co.uk/ ww1lives/**.
>
> It is always worth searching for the book on the internet as in some cases it may be available online. *A history of South Cave and of other parishes in the East Riding of the county of York* contains names of many people who lived and worked in the local villages and is available on the free archive.org website: **https://archive.org/details/ historyofsouthca00hall/page/n5/mode/2up**. If the book is not freely available online, a local researcher will be able to access it if you cannot.
>
> *Anne Sherman QG® PG(Dip), Qualified Genealogist, Leaves Family History Research Services:* **https://leavesfamilyhistory.co.uk**

And of course, don't discount the possibility of carrying out some of your research with the help of others and maybe enlist a professional further down the line. Forums, chat rooms, social media and Q&A seasons can all offer the opportunity to ask questions and share knowledge. Family history journals and magazines such as *Family Tree* and *Who Do You Think You Are?* also offer 'problem' pages, although these are often over-subscribed and so you may wait a while for a reply.

Courses and Talks

Gone are the days when gaining family history knowledge meant travelling to your nearest college after a long day at work. The Covid-19 pandemic saw so many societies, learning providers and archives go online with their offerings, giving you the option for anything from a one-hour talk to a full qualification that can take several years to complete.

For Yorkshire-themed learning, check out what county and local archives are offering, and don't overlook libraries. The events programme of the relevant family history society for the area in which your ancestors lived can be a rich source of learning; even where some events have returned to an on-site format, online attendance is still often an option as societies offer hybrid events to cater for their non-local audiences.

Legacy Family Tree Webinars offers a free programme of talks throughout the year and whilst few of these are Yorkshire-themed, they do offer skills and topics that would benefit your research wherever you live: **https://familytreewebinars.com**. You can either catch the webinars live or watch in the website's library. Every September, the Webtember programme offers live and pre-recorded webinars for each day of the month.

RootsTech is an annual genealogy conference, billed as the world's biggest such gathering, taking place each March. After the pandemic it ran in an online-only format and even after its move to a hybrid event, offers many hours of digital content. The best way to get involved is to sign up in the weeks before the event, by visiting **www.familysearch.org/en/rootstech** and registering for free. You'll then be given the conference dates and can register for the sessions that interest you. Previous events have had Yorkshire- and England-based content, and you can create your own playlist and enjoy the talks freely for a year after broadcast. Another interesting benefit is the 'relatives at RootsTech' tool, which you'll be introduced to as part of your registration journey. This allows you to add your family tree to FamilySearch as a Gedcom file and then find out which of your relatives are also attending RootsTech. These will likely be people you've never heard of, from other countries, with whom you share at least one ancestor.

For longer-term learning, Pharos Tutors **www.pharostutors.com** offers a range of courses on various topics, as does Society of Genealogists,

Every year, thousands of genealogists visit Salt Lake City in Utah for RootsTech, which is also streamed online. (© William Henry Jackson)

with the latter opening most of its talks and classes to non-members **https://societyofgenealogists.arlo.co/w/**. Be sure to check whether the talk is recorded if broadcast live, as you can often re-watch or view the recording if you couldn't attend the live broadcast.

If you'd like to take your skills a step further, you might want to consider gaining a qualification, whether to enhance your skills or as a step towards becoming a qualified genealogist and possibly advising others. The Institute of Heraldic and Genealogical Studies **www.ihgs.ac.uk/courselist** runs distance learning courses throughout the year, as does University of Strathclyde with its online genealogical research programme **www.strath.ac.uk/studywithus/centreforlifelonglearning/genealogy/** at which you can study from an eight-week beginner course through to post-graduate level.

Volunteering

This section covers some of the many ways you can offer your services as a family history volunteer from the comfort of your own home. Whether you're helping your nearest family history society to transcribe information for a new online database, or volunteering on a global DNA project, there are many ways to get involved, no matter what your skill level.

Why volunteer?
What are the benefits of volunteering within the family history world and why do people do this? For some, it's a way of giving back to the community; think of the many hundreds of datasets that you've browsed since you started to build your family tree – much of the information you've used will have been gathered by volunteers.

For others, working on a project allows for great digital interaction with others, and that feeling of being part of something bigger. And of course, you might be lucky enough to be able to work with information that hasn't yet been released to the public.

What skills are needed?
The skills you need will vary from project to project, but you might be surprised at how little is needed on many projects, where a willingness to copy information from one format to another with accuracy could be all that's needed. For other work, you may be able to get the training 'on the job' as you progress with the work, perhaps working online with a project partner.

Volunteer projects

So, how can you find out what opportunities are available? In many cases, it's just a matter of keeping your eyes and ears open. Register for e-mail updates for societies, forums and archives of which you're a member and keep an eye on their social media channels too. If you receive a journal from your genealogy society, they may issue regular calls for volunteers.

Yorkshire Burials **https://yorkshireburials.uk** are always happy to welcome volunteers for their ongoing transcription projects. As we explored in Chapters 1 and 6, this growing database needs people 'on the ground' who can visit burial grounds to record monumental inscriptions and take photos. At the time of writing, the site owners told me that some of the major cemeteries in Leeds still require more photographs, including Beckett Street, Holbeck, Killingbeck and Hunslet. Volunteers are also used to transcribe parish and municipal burial records to add to more than 1 million records on the website. Visit **https://yorkshireburials.uk** and complete the 'contact us' form to find out more.

In a similar vein, Sheffield Indexers **www.sheffieldindexers.com/AboutIndex.html** is a group of volunteers who work to create free-to-use material for the benefit of the whole genealogy community. The current projects are indexing both burial records and parish records for Sheffield, whilst a trade directories dataset also continues to be updated, and there is also an ongoing BMD certificate project. Or if you're not ready for volunteer status just yet, you can help in another way by uploading copies of Sheffield birth, marriage and death certificates from your own collections to help other researchers (and potential distant cousins who may be researching the same ancestors).

On a wider scale, Free BMD, Free CEN and FamilySearch regularly enlist the help of volunteers for long-term projects. The former two send you images to transcribe, links to the software needed (or to a pre-formatted spreadsheet) and guidance on how to transcribe. FamilySearch volunteer opportunities are here **www.familysearch.org/en/info/volunteer** and range from offering your services as a research volunteer, to translating genealogical material from one language into another.

And finally, a form of volunteering via donation that I thought worth a mention. The West Yorkshire Archive Service runs a scheme where you can sponsor a box from their wide-ranging and well-regarded John Goodchild Collection, one of the county's largest collections amassed by one individual. Money raised from the sponsorship goes towards the preservation, packaging, cataloguing and conservation work needed to ensure that the collection is available and accessible for all. You can find out more and download a leaflet at **www.wyjs.org.uk/archive-service/our-collections/the-john-goodchild-collection/**.

If volunteering isn't right for you at the moment or you simply don't have the time, take comfort in the fact that simply by ensuring any information you input to your publicly accessible tree is accurate and honest, then you are doing your own small bit for the family history community's present and future researchers.

Chapter 10

ADDING COLOUR TO YOUR RESEARCH

So, you've tracked your ancestors from cradle to grave, using a range of records and websites – what next? This chapter takes us through the many different ways you can add colour to your research by using resources such as maps, old photographs, historical directories and a range of immersive websites to flesh out your research.

As we've seen, family history is so much more than simply names and dates on a family tree; our ancestors only really come to life when we can picture the places they lived, their surroundings, and what their home life would have been like.

Old Photographs

Whilst photos of individual ancestors are the holy grail of the family history world, you can also enrich your existing collections of individuals and groups with other photos that relate to the world in which your forebears lived.

Think about their surroundings: from the individual house and street, on through to the area and to the level of town or village and challenge yourself to find photos, drawings or paintings of local landmarks.

The main Yorkshire archives all have great online image collections and East Yorkshire is particularly well served.

The East Riding Archives What Was Here site **https://whatwashere.org/map/** is a really fun and engaging way to explore this area of the county through old photos. Begin with the modern-day numbered map, select your place of interest (you can even search by address) and then click to see old photos of the area. These archive images can then be overlaid on maps dating from the 1600s to 1800s.

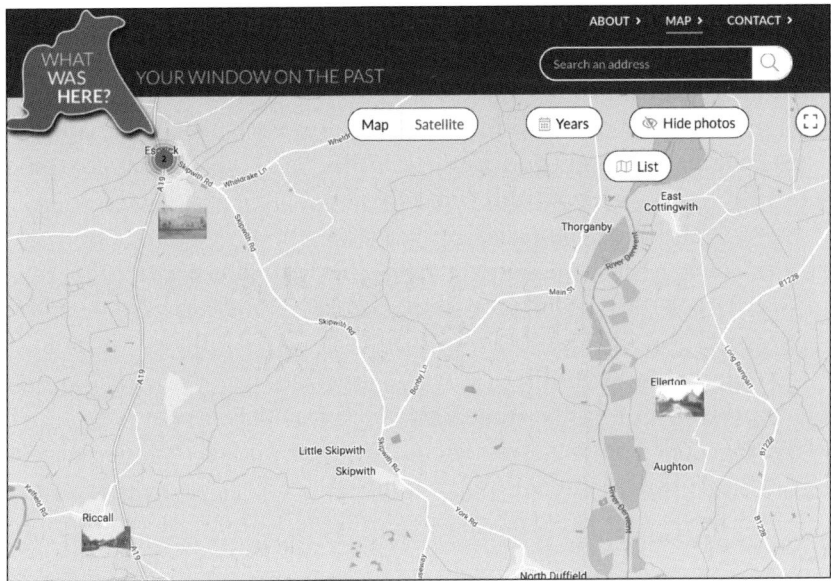

Use What Was Here? to compare then and now East Riding views.

Staying in East Yorkshire, the Preservica Digital Archive **https://eastriding.access.preservica.com** allows you to search and view digital archives, including videos, oral history recordings, photographs and documents. Although the site mainly relates to the more recent past, it does contain some digitised records of older material.

Finally, East Riding Photos **https://picturearchives.org/eastridingphotos** allows you to browse and order prints of historical scenes from your ancestor's town or village.

For West Yorkshire, the Twixt Aire and Calder photo archive **www.twixtaireandcalder.org.uk** covers Wakefield and district, plus associated areas. As well as old photos, it offers maps, memorabilia and prints.

Sheffield City Council Archives' Picture Sheffield **www.picturesheffield.com** has over 100,000 images, with new photos and documents regularly added, and stretches from the Victorian Age through to the Covid-19 pandemic. From images of sports events and Morris dancers, through to the work of the city's cutlers and railwaymen, you can search by keyword or topic and also create your own themed albums on the site.

Explore York Archives' York Images **https://exploreyork.org.uk/archives/york-images/** runs along similar lines, with almost 8,000 images collected under the themes of 'people', 'places' and 'events'. The latter is particularly immersive as it's easy to imagine that our ancestors would have enjoyed watching, or even taking part in, the historical pageants that were so popular in the 1920s, enjoying a funfair at the city park, setting up a street party for a royal event, or gathering with friends and family for the opening of a civic building. Such events would have been talked about and preparations made for weeks beforehand and afterwards and were part of the fabric of everyday life.

Moving on from landmarks, you can add further context with photos of military uniforms, everyday workwear for a particular period of time, even examples of what a typical home of the era would have looked like.

Create a digital scrapbook
One way to bring your research to life is to hunt down old photographs of the area your forebears lived and worked. Even if you can't find photos of the exact house or even street, you'll perhaps find the mill where they worked, a postcard of the town from around that time, or photographs of workers dressed in the same garb they would have worn.

If you're using the photos purely for your own research and pleasure, you should be able to find plenty of copyright-free options. Some of my favourites are Tuck DB Postcards **https://tuckdbpostcards.org**, Wellcome Collection images **https://wellcomecollection.org/images** and The Met New York **www.metmuseum.org/art/collection/search**. The main subscription family history sites also have images, and it's always worth checking the website of the family history society for the town your ancestor called home.

Memory Lane **www.memorylane.co.uk** has over 15,000 photos, from 1878 onwards and over 1,000 of these are from Yorkshire. However, if you're looking for nostalgia rather than geographical area, try browsing categories such as transport, seasonal and military.

Leodis is a similar format, but devoted entirely to the city of Leeds and surrounds, with 68,000+ images: **www.leodis.net**. As well as searching by keyword (street name, district, etc.) there is a pot luck section, which is fun to browse, and a 'can you help?' area where members of the public are asked to submit information to help identify some of the photos. A lot of the images are owned by Leeds Libraries but many belong to other heritage organisations and individuals. The site can be searched by keyword or you can browse for a certain area. Leodis is free to use and you can create an account to add comments to photos or to order reproductions.

The above is a snapshot of what's available, but most towns and villages have online collections and also don't forget auction websites such as eBay or specialised postcard retailers, as well as a general web search. When you begin to explore, you might be pleasantly surprised to discover that no matter how small a town, village or even street, how seemingly off the tourist trail it may seem to have been, it could well still feature on an old postcard. As the text messages of their day, postcards were sent in their hundreds of thousands in their Victorian and Edwardian heyday, and not just from those staying at seaside resorts. Soldiers announcing a return from duty, children on a school trip, business men and women communicating with colleagues were just some of those who sent picture postcards.

Film
Seeing your ancestors on film does, of course, add a whole new dimension to your research. However, unless you're lucky enough to have inherited family film reels, your experience may have to be restricted to seeing the places and events your ancestors might have experienced.

The oldest surviving film in existence was actually filmed in Yorkshire, at Oakwood Grange in Roundhay, by Frenchman Louis Le Prince in 1888. A second film, *Traffic Crossing Leeds Bridge*, was recorded eighteen months later. Excerpts from each of these can be seen on Wikipedia: **https://en.wikipedia.org/wiki/Louis_Le_Prince**.

The Yorkshire/North East Film Archive **www.yfanefa.com/about** is the perfect place to expand your family history research into moving images. The site has 70,000 film tapes covering 130 years, with hundreds of hours' worth of free-to-use content that you can browse, focusing on your interests. For example, you might want to search for films relating to an ancestor's town or village, footage of a particular craft or occupation, or celebrations such as pageants or parades.

Although the films available online are described by the archive as 'just a taster' of the full, diverse collection, they are nevertheless wide ranging and valuable. The archive is actively collecting new material on an ongoing basis and so is worth bookmarking to check every so often. You can also register at **https://bit.ly/3UfTF41** for a quarterly newsletter that advises of new accessions and shares curated film clips.

British Pathé, once a familiar name to twentieth-century cinema goers, also has an extensive online archive at **www.britishpathe.com**, many of which relate to notable news events that our ancestors would have read about or been involved in, such as royal visits, motorbike races, ship launches and sporting events. The 'heritage hub' section of the site is also worth a look, with full-length films on more general topics including biographies, twentieth-century history and the two world wars.

YouTube is another great source, particularly for twentieth-century film clips featuring local traditions and old occupations. Some archives have their own channels on here, including East Yorkshire Archives, whose collection includes brief clips from raw archive footage, mainly relating to the town of Beverley: **https://bit.ly/3Lx2baH**.

In 'archive to armchair', East Riding archivist Hannah Stamp takes viewers on a tour around mid-twentieth-century East Riding scenes. These are stills rather than video footage and the presentation is very engaging, beginning in Beverley and then moving outwards to surrounding villages. All of the documents featured in the three-minute film can be found at the archives: **https://bit.ly/3AWpjfc**. In a similar format, Sound Cloud also has a selection of local music and history recordings, also from East Riding Archives: **https://soundcloud.com/eastridingarchives**. The selections focusing on local dialects are particularly interesting as, of course, this topic lends itself very well to sound recordings.

Maps

The most obvious use for historical maps is to locate an ancestor's residence, street or town. But this is just the first step, as you can then enrich your understanding by looking at the surrounding area on the map and seeing churches, places of leisure, workplaces and transport hubs. It's also very interesting to seek out maps for the period before and after your ancestor lived in a place, to get an understanding of how the place changed over the years. Seeing that a town had expanded quickly in the decades after your ancestor arrived, or that they lived there in the years before a major employer left and the settlement shrank, allows you to understand more.

Historical maps are perfect to use in digitised form, since many original maps can be fragile and irreplaceable, yet when viewed on screen you can magnify and manipulate them to your heart's content.

Yorkshire has many online map resources and I'm starting with perhaps somewhere you might not initially think to look. National Library of Scotland is an unlikely sounding place to find Yorkshire maps but is one of the best free online sites for the UK. The site **https://maps.nls.uk** has over 250,000 maps and is easy and fun to use.

The attractive home page allows you to do a traditional keyword search, or browse by type of map, mapmaker, county maps, town plans, etc. You can also view maps side by side, to see how an area changed, e.g. with the coming of industry, the arrival of a railway line, a new housing estate appearing – any of which could really impact an ancestor's life.

Map Finder is a good place to get your bearings. Type in a place name or address on the top left and you'll be given a modern map, with a choice of other historical maps shown on the right-hand side of the screen. Click on to these and explore the street names, pubs, mills, etc. As you go back in time, closely packed streets become farmers' fields. Or perhaps it could be the other way round, as a once bustling metropolis was sidelined by the opening of a railway in a nearby town, causing a drop in population.

You can use local maps for tracing how street names change over the years, particularly if you 'lose' a street when tracing through the census. Sometimes a street was initially named after one developer then when it was redeveloped decades later, was renamed.

Another useful tool on this site is the 'side by side' option, where you can locate an ancestor's home and then compare this to a modern-day aerial view on the same screen, to see whether the place still exists.

The Tithe Maps website **http://wytithemaps.org.uk** was created by the West Yorkshire Archive Service and provides free access to the tithe maps of the Bradford and Leeds districts. These maps and accompanying documents, created between the 1830s and 1860s, captured the district at the start of the Industrial Revolution and will show you who lived in your area of interest, who owned the land in question, and the use to which the land was put. You can delight in seeing down to the scale of an individual field, wood, river or stream. These large-scale maps are

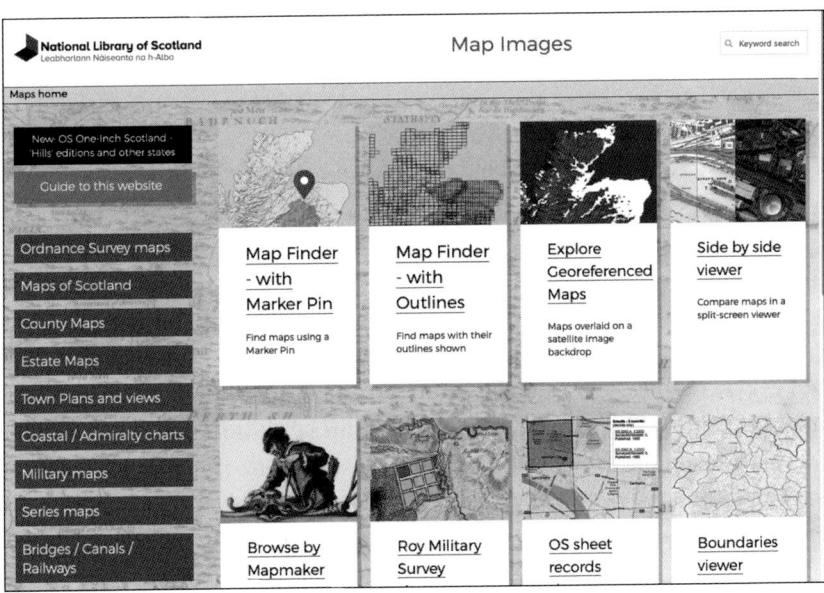

The National Library of Scotland maps home page.

accompanied by documents called apportionments, which show who owned and occupied each plot, and even give the name of individual fields.

The home page presents the maps with the place names in alphabetical order and you then click on to your chosen place to see the map and accompanying apportionment, with the latter opening separately as an Excel spreadsheet. You can choose to 'click full screen map' for an immersive experience with the map presented on your screen, or leave in original view to have a modern-day map to refer to alongside your historical map. If you're interested in a particular plot on the tithe map, simply note its number and then open the Excel spreadsheet, where you'll find the forename and surname of both owner and occupier (sometimes the same person), the associated premises, the state of cultivation of the land and the extent of the land holding.

Archive Maps **https://treasurehousemaps.eastriding.gov.uk** from East Riding Archives allows visitors to browse the archives' holdings of historical Ordnance Survey maps from 1855 to 1929. Old Maps Online **www.oldmapsonline.org** fulfils a similar role but covers a wider date range. Here, you can start your search by place name or region and after pressing 'search' will be presented with a number of maps of various dates and then click on the one you'd like to study. Many of the resulting maps are from the National Library of Scotland maps collections mentioned above.

And finally, FamilySearch Maps **www.familysearch.org/mapp/** is separate to the main FamilySearch site. On this database, simply type in your place of interest and when your results are returned, if your place is listed as 'other places' alongside its main entry this indicates that this settlement has records in more than one area – it used to belong to another parish, for example – and so you may need to search those records, depending on your year or area of interest. Once you click the map, the 'info' tab gives the non-Church of England denominations covered, years for the parish records, whilst the 'jurisdictions' is hugely helpful as a tab with details of which civil registration district, probate court, poor law union and more – all of potential help for tracking down certain records.

One final map set that can't easily be found online but is worth knowing about is the Goad maps that run from the eighteenth century onwards. They are named after Charles E. Goad who was born in Surrey and worked as a cartographer in Montreal in the 1870s. His detailed UK city maps began when he returned in 1885. These were insurance maps, showing things such as the material from which a building was constructed, its nearest water source etc. and they were used to help insurers to make decisions about premiums charged. Many town libraries and county archives have these types of maps and they tend to be very large. To date, I haven't been able to find any for Yorkshire to access online apart from the Goad Street Maps (£) where you can buy copies for various UK towns and cities.

Newspapers

Outside of the birth, marriage and death announcements, which you may have used to help you in tracing out the paths of your ancestors' lives, newspapers can also be used to flesh out your research, both in terms of finding mentions of an ancestor's sporting appearances, prizes at local fetes and galas and also in building up a picture of the local and national news scene at a given time.

When starting your searches, do bear in mind that many newspapers, particularly before the twentieth century, only printed an initial rather than forename, and some only used a married woman's husband's name, e.g. Mrs Jack Baker.

As well as exploring local stories involving your ancestors, newspapers are always a mirror of their time and as such, the headlines for any particular month and year can show you what international, national and local matters people might have been discussing over the breakfast table, at the pub and in the workplace. Times of hardship, celebration,

Denby Dale, early 20th century. (© Tuck DB Postcards)

failed harvests and economic booms are all chronicled and commented upon, with the letters pages acting as a barometer of public opinion.

Finding a newspaper notice, however minor, featuring an ancestor is a brief window into that person's life in between those milestones of birth, marriage, death and of course, the census. Seeing an ancestor named, for example, as a creditor, the recipient of an award, or even as the subject of an insolvency notice, shows you his or her presence at a particular point in time, and can often act as reassurance that this person was still alive, even if perhaps not thriving in some cases. For such purposes, *The Gazette* **www.thegazette.co.uk** is a good starting point, as the home of more than three centuries' worth of public notices. The site is free to use and also offers a paid-for research service.

Keep an eye, too, on newspaper reports of local events such as industrial accidents, motoring incidents, thefts and so on. Even if your ancestor wasn't the perpetrator or victim, their words and actions as a witness might have been reported, either at the scene or later in court. *The Huddersfield Chronicle*'s 'Thirsk Disaster' report (on British Newspaper Archive) of 3 December 1892 is a case in point. Following a railway accident involving the Scotch Express, several men were called upon to give evidence as to the actions of signalman James Holmes, who had been charged with manslaughter:

> Evidence was also given by Dr J. S. Walton, Dr Tempest-Anderson, Thomas Kirkby stationmaster; Joseph Barnes, driver of the goods train, Henry Eden, signalman at Otterington; Thomas Gibson, signalman at Avenue Junction; George Bean, guard of the Scotch express; Edward Heads, fireman of the express; Thomas Pickering, and Inspector Cook … The accused was committed to take his trail at the assizes, bail being allowed … The chairman complimented George Bean, the guard, for his presence of mind in blocking the line and rendering assistance to the passengers.

The British Newspaper Archive (BNA) **www.britishnewspaperarchive.co.uk** is home to an ever-growing collection of more than three centuries of historical newspapers, many of which are free to access. Within this project, 2 million free pages are available to explore, with the BNA committed to digitising 5 million pages within the next five years. If you want to find only free-of-charge images, you'll firstly need to create a free account. Then, enter your search term into the box in the centre of the home page and then when your results are returned, scroll down the left-hand column and tick 'free to view'. This filter also works if you choose to browse by date, place, name, etc.

The site has more than seventy Yorkshire titles to explore, the oldest of which is the *Leeds Intelligencer*, first printed on one of the city's main streets, The Headrow, by Griffith Wright in 1754. If you wish to explore beyond the scope of the free-to-access pages, you can take a monthly, quarterly or annual subscription

Start your search on the home page **www.britishnewspaperarchive. co.uk** and if you wish, you can choose a region of Yorkshire (north, south, east or west) but do bear in mind that news from one area of the region might make it into another, so unless searching for a very common name or place, a wider search might be better initially.

Alternatively, if you'd like to add some local colour to your research, try a search with the place name and year when your ancestor would have been located there. Some of my maternal Leeds ancestors lived in the centre of town in the 1750s and might well have read about – or even travelled on – the 'flying machine' stage that was described in the *Sheffield Public Advertiser* on 17 May 1763:

> **The Leeds Flying Machine**
> Sets out from Nottingham every Wednesday, Friday and Monday Mornings; Breakfasts at Mansfield, Dines at Sheffield, and lies at Leeds. Sets out from the Old King's Arms at Leeds, every Tuesday, Thursday, and Saturday Mornings …
>
> No Writings, Jewels, Plates or Cash, will be answered for, unless entered as such, and paid for accordingly.
>
> To be performed as God permit by,
> JOHN HANDFORTH
> SAMUEL GLANVILLE, and
> WILLIAM RICHARDSON

You can also access indexed newspaper collections via the main commercial family history providers. In many cases a newspaper report would be presented to you when searching for a particular ancestor within a specific time frame, but you can also filter the results to receive only newspaper results, or begin your search within that provider's newspaper collection.

Oral History
As family historians, we are often very involved in working with the written word and, if we're lucky, old photographs. However, oral histories

and sound recordings can provide a rich insight into old customs, words and even accents. Oral history lends itself well to online study, as many of the recordings made over the years have been digitised or at least transcribed.

Many of these collections were gathered as the result of a project to gather, or sometimes record, interviews with people on a specific topic such as coal mining, a historic event or old customs. Although many of these collections are available only by visiting a library or archive, there are some that can be enjoyed online, such as the Changing Horizons project on people's memories of coastal change and the fishing industry in the East Riding: **https://bit.ly/44IUZB5**. This page gives links to a thirty-minute YouTube film and three-minute trailer.

British Library Sounds is a gem, with plenty of Yorkshire material, including a Water, Steel and Energy collection: **https://sounds.bl.uk/ Oral-history/Industry-water-steel-and-energy**. When searching the collections, no matter what your keyword(s) tick the 'search the recordings anyone can play' box to access all recordings available to you online. You can also create themed playlists and favourites collections.

Oral history is a vibrant field and, as such, projects are usually underway somewhere in the county. Keep an eye on the news section of the Oral History Society's Yorkshire page **www.ohs.org.uk/regions/ yorkshire/** where you'll find progress reports and news of project launches and completions.

Cheapside, Barnsley, c.1904. (© Tuck DB Postcards)

One-Place Studies

If exploring your ancestor's wider world has fired up your imagination, consider undertaking a one-place study, or even just exploring to see whether anyone else has studied your town or village of interest. Digging into the history of a particular place not only helps you to flesh out the wider picture of your ancestor's life it can even help break down brick walls, as many such studies will lead you to record sets that you might not have come across during traditional family history research.

The beauty of a study of this nature is that it can be as formal or informal as you like. You can register your project with The Society for One-Place Studies (**www.one-place-studies.org**) so that others can take part or share information; or you can simply carry out the research for your own benefit and pleasure. You could study a whole village, street or even property. Some towns and villages have their own Facebook or Instagram page dedicated to the history of that place, and these often have great photo collections to browse and the opportunity to ask questions, get help with labelling photos etc.

In a similar vein, the One Place Studies Directory **https://oneplacestudy.org** has over 200 studies for the county. Many of these lead to some real gems such as studies of a particular area and its genealogy, or collections of old photos also things such as house histories, graveyard studies etc.

Although there is no set way to carry out a one-place study, it's worth considering the size of the settlement that you intend to study before you make a start. Firstly, check The Society for One-Place Studies (above) to see whether anyone else is studying the same place. If so, you can either avoid duplicating your efforts by working together, or you might decide to try a different ancestral place. If the place you're considering is large (say over 5,000 inhabitants) you could narrow down by studying a particular area, suburb or even an individual street. You might be surprised at how much you could discover about a single street through the use of the census, trade directories, local newspapers, photo collections and so on.

Name and Place **www.nameandplace.com** (£) is a data management and mapping app exclusively designed for one-place studies, one-name studies and other local history projects. The software is different from most others in that it assigns equal weight to both person and place. For example, you might record an ancestor's baptism in a particular church and then you can also record all relevant baptisms in that church, and view the data from either viewpoint. You can also record all places relevant to you, down to the level of an individual gravestone. So one-name, one-place and even one-building studies are all possible.

> **British Association for Local History**
> If you've enjoyed finding out more about your ancestor's town or village, you might want to take things further and join the society nearest to where your forebears lived. The British Association for Local History **www.balh.org.uk/societies-az** has a society directory accessible from its home page with well over 100 Yorkshire groups listed. These range from civic societies, through antiquarian groups and on to local history groups, with the latter probably most similar to family history groups in their set up and events programmes. The talks, slide shows and publications that local history societies offer can often contain material and knowledge it could be impossible to find elsewhere and since the pandemic, many of these groups offer online or hybrid meetings.

Many of the country's libraries and archives have blogs or website sections relating to the history of a particular area. For example, the Secret Library Leeds blog, which is added to each week and focuses on the collections housed in Leeds Libraries: **https://secretlibraryleeds.net/**. There is a Family History tab at the top of the page which brings all Leeds Libraries research and collection guides together in one place. Topics cover all areas of family history and highlight both digital and printed records. The Research and Collections Guides tab may also be of interest.

One-Name Studies

A one-name study concentrates on all instances of a surname within a specific geographical area – ranging from a small settlement to a whole county or country. One reason for doing this is that if you can work out patterns in surname distribution, you might be able to find your way through a family history problem such as an ancestor who seems to 'disappear' from the records. Knowing where a particular family name is concentrated can help you decide where to focus your search next and perhaps help you to work out whether and why an ancestor moved from one area to another.

Many surnames have their own society dedicated to the history and study of that name and you don't have to be carrying out a study project to join; an interest in the name is sufficient. Many of these societies are listed with the Guild of One-Name Studies **https://one-name.org** and this site has a surname search. The Guild has its own Yorkshire branch, which runs regional meetings and talks, to which non-members are welcome.

These groups range from large to small and can provide you with specialised help and access to online databases that you would not be able to access elsewhere. For example, as mentioned previously, Metcalfe is a Yorkshire name and the society **www.metcalfes-online.co.uk/metcalfeorg/** is one of the UK's biggest such groups. As an example of member benefits, you not only a bi-monthly newsletter but also gain access to a growing database of 100,000 names, as well as the opportunity to submit your family tree to be checked by society experts and a report returned to you.

The Midgley One-Name Study site **http://midgleywebpages.com** is another such group and this website is divided into different sections geographically within the county, focusing on instances of the surname in mostly West Yorkshire locations including Bradford, Halifax, Thornton and Todmorden. The site explains that many of those who carry this name descend from people who made their living from wool produced on the Pennine moors and then traded along Yorkshire's packhorse routes and down the Great North Road at Doncaster.

These groups are also a great way to make contact with others studying the same surname which, depending on the rarity of the name, might also be the same family line as you.

ACKNOWLEDGEMENTS

When writing this book, I was lucky enough to be able to enlist advice, tips and support from genealogy professionals across Yorkshire. I apologise if I've missed anyone from the following list and I'd also like to pay tribute to the many un-named volunteers and employees who have helped to make archive material available online over the years.

Special thanks go to Margaret Boustead, North Yorkshire County Record Office; Steven Bruce, Yorkshire Family History; Else Churchill, Society of Genealogists; Jennifer Brierley, West Yorkshire Archives Service; Laura Gardiner, Rotherham Archives; Jo Heron and The Metcalfe Society; Jess Hogg, Doncaster Archives; Paul Joiner, Joiner Marriage Index; Anne Sherman, Leaves Family History Research Services; Graeme Siddall and Sheffield Archives; Helen Skilbeck, Leeds Central Library; Hannah Stamp and East Riding Archives; Second World War Experience Centre; Paul Stebbing, Barnsley Archives; Sue Steel and Bradford Family History Society; Nick Thorne, TheGenealogist; Peter Thorpe and Karen Baker, National Railway Museum; Steve Whitwam; Mike and Steve, Yorkshire Burials; Laura Yeoman, The Borthwick Institute for Archives.

INDEX

Ancestry website, 12

Barnsley archives, 7
Bastardy records, 32
Bolton Abbey, 24, 77
Borthwick Institute for Archives, 4, 9, 31, 57, 68, 82
Bradford, 4, 60, 65, 67, 75–6, 92–3, 101, 108, 127, 135
Bradford Family History Society, 108
Bradford Local Studies Library, 108
Bradford Historical Society, 51

Census 34–8, 98–9
Census substitutes, 38–9
County record offices, 4
Courses, 118–19
Crime 65–9

Dade Registers, 23
Deed registers, 41–2
Discovery catalogue, 3
Doncaster, 7, 135
Doncaster archives, 4, 6–7, 15

East Riding of Yorkshire archives, 5, 64
Education, 7, 45–7, 60, 67, 77, 80
Emigration, 10–16

FamilySearch website, 13
FindMyPast website, 15

Film 125–6
Fishing, 47, 54–5, 132
FreeBMD website, 15

Halifax, 4, 10, 17, 42, 46, 67, 135
Holidays, 77–8
House history, 43–4
Huddersfield Family History Society, 17
Hull History Centre, 4–5, 42, 82
Hull Local Studies Library, 6
Hull City Archives, 4, 6, 54

Immigration, 12, 95–104

Kirklees, 8, 17, 53
Kirklees Cousins, 53, 59, 113

Land tax, 41
Leeds, 4, 8, 11, 29–31, 39, 65, 67, 72–3, 75–6, 111–12, 120, 124, 127, 131, 134
Liddle Collection, 59

Manorial Documents Register, 42
Manorial records, 17, 42–3
Maps, 6–7, 16, 22, 42–3, 48, 60, 75, 100, 113, 122–3, 126–9
Military 56–9
Mining, 12, 47, 51–3, 59, 132
MyHeritage website, 16

National Coal Mining Museum, 53
National Media Museum, 75

National Railway Museum, 61
Newspapers, 129–31
North Yorkshire Archives, 6
North Yorkshire County record office, 15, 23, 42, 66

Occupations, 47–52, 90–2
One-name studies, 134–5
One-place studies, 133–34
Oral history, 89–90

Parish chest records, 32–3
Picture Sheffield, 8, 66, 74, 89, 123
Poverty 62–5, 86–7
Prison records, 69–70
Professional research, 114–17
Property deeds, 7, 52–3
Protests, 87–9

Railways, 54, 60–1, 63, 71
Rate books 40–41
Religion, 12, 71, 78–80
Rotherham, 4, 6, 8, 58
  archives, 58
  Clifton Park Museum, 58

Saltaire, 60, 91, 101
Scarborough, 54–5, 71, 77
Scarborough Maritime Heritage Centre, 55
Second World War Experience Centre, 59
Sheffield, 4, 6, 8, 15, 63, 66–7, 76, 80, 101, 113, 120, 131
Sheffield archives, 6, 8, 15, 123
Sheffield Libraries, 89
Sheffield Local Studies Library, 60, 72–4, 148
Sport, 76
Strays, 95–6

Textiles, 12, 35, 47, 51–3, 60, 65, 76, 86, 90, 93, 95, 97, 99, 101–102
TheGenealogist website, 15

Trade directories, 39, 44–5, 47–8, 74–5, 120, 133
  Bradford, 108

University of Bradford, J B Priestley Library, 44, 149
University of Hull archives, 6, 42, 82
University of Leeds Brotherton Library (special collections), 9, 30, 59
University of Sheffield, 76

Volunteering, 119–21

Wakefield Court Rolls, 9, 69
West Riding Registry of Deeds, 41
West Yorkshire archive service, 4, 8–9, 17, 31–2, 41, 58, 64, 67, 120, 127
West Yorkshire Archive Service, Bradford, 4, 8, 108, 127
West Yorkshire Archive Service, Calderdale, 8
West Yorkshire Archive Service, Huddersfield, 4
West Yorkshire Archive Service, Kirklees, 8, 17
West Yorkshire Archive Service, Leeds, 31
West Yorkshire Archive Service, Wakefield, 4, 8, 13, 41
Whitby Abbey, 74
Wills, 17, 30–2, 50, 92, 111
Workhouse, 16, 38, 63–6, 86–7
  Ripon Workhouse Museum, 87

York City archives, 15, 123
York Family History Society, 111
York Registry, 31
Yorkshire Archaeological Society, 4, 9, 29, 69, 109
Yorkshire Film Archive, 55, 60, 76–7, 125

Dear Reader,

We hope you have enjoyed this book, but why not share your views on social media? You can also follow our pages to see more about our other products: facebook.com/penandswordbooks or follow us on Twitter @penswordbooks

You can also view our products at www.pen-and-sword.co.uk (UK and ROW) or www.penandswordbooks.com (North America).

To keep up to date with our latest releases and online catalogues, please sign up to our newsletter at: www.pen-and-sword.co.uk/newsletter

If you would like a printed catalogue with our latest books, then please email: enquiries@pen-and-sword.co.uk or telephone: 01226 734555 (UK and ROW) or email: uspen-and-sword@casematepublishers.com or telephone: (610) 853-9131 (North America).

We respect your privacy and we will only use personal information to send you information about our products.

Thank you!